NAZI SABOTEURS

SABO

Hitler's Secret

NAZI TEURS

Attack on America

Samantha Seiple

SCHOLASTIC
FOCUS
New York

Library of Congress Cataloging-in-Publication Data

Names: Seiple, Samantha, author.
Title: Nazi saboteurs : Hitler's secret attack on America / Samantha Seiple.
Description: First edition. | New York, NY : Scholastic Focus, [2019] | Audience:
    Ages: 8 to 12. | Includes bibliographical references.
Identifiers: LCCN 2018054402 (print) | LCCN 2019000901 (ebook) |
    ISBN 9781338259247 (Ebook) | ISBN 9781338259148 (hardcover : alk. paper) |
    ISBN 9781338259193 (pbk. : alk. paper)
Subjects: LCSH: World War, 1939-1945—Secret service—Germany—Juvenile
    literature. | Espionage, German—United States—History—20th century—
    Juvenile literature. | Sabotage—United States—History—20th century—Juvenile
    literature. | Spies—Germany—Biography—Juvenile literature. | Nazis—
    United States—Biography—Juvenile literature.
Classification: LCC D810.S7 (ebook) | LCC D810.S7 S386 2019 (print) |
    DDC 940.54/87430973—dc23

10 9 8 7 6 5 4 3 2 1   19 20 21 22 23

Printed in the U.S.A.   23
First edition, December 2019

Book design by Abby Dening

For Todd

Table of Contents

THE WATCHMAN

June 13, 1942
(Six months after Adolf Hitler declared
war on the United States and one week
after the Japanese invaded Alaska)

It was past midnight in the seaside fishing village of Amagansett, on the East End of Long Island, New York, and a stubborn fog cloaked the town's ribbon of beach. The murky visibility was making it nearly impossible for rookie coast guardsman John Cullen to do his job.

Cullen was a "beach pounder," and one of his duties was patrolling the three-mile stretch of desolate shoreline for any suspicious activity. Three weeks before, the U.S. Army had issued a warning of a possible enemy submarine landing. But no one knew when or where it would happen along the 2,000 mile Atlantic coastline between Maine and Florida. So far, every night was always the same. Cullen never saw anyone or anything.

Armed with just a flashlight and flare gun, Cullen continued to walk and patrol the shoreline. The tide was low, and the waves were rolling in and crashing down angrily, sending a thin sheet of foamy salt water over the packed sand. He walked along the water's edge, where it felt like a spongy sidewalk under his feet. After six months on the job, Cullen knew it was inevitable that the sand would creep into his socks despite the canvas gaiters covering his pant legs and shoes.

The thick fog washed over him. The dewy drops clung like lint to his neatly pressed uniform and dripped down his neck from his closely shorn hair. It was so dark and the fog was so thick that he couldn't even see his shiny military-issued shoes. He also couldn't see the German submarine a quarter of a mile away from the shoreline. Or the Nazi saboteurs in a rubber boat filled with explosives bobbing in the water not twenty feet away from him.

Before his job as a sand pounder, Cullen had worked as a deliveryman for Macy's department store in New York City. His former employer described him as "a thoroughly wholesome, typically American boy" with a "modest demeanor." Cullen had decided to quit his job to join the Coast Guard after the Japanese bombed Pearl Harbor.

By the time Cullen arrived in Amagansett, Americans had begun to feel the deprivations of war. "Dim-out" rules had been put into effect, so Cullen saw no lights twinkling anywhere in the misty darkness. At first, people had resisted turning out their lights at sundown, but they were warned that the police would take action, especially against any motorists who drove with their headlights shining like a lighthouse beacon along the coast. The blackout helped protect the U.S. ships that were out at sea, patrolling the coast for any lurking German U-boats.

Despite the recent rationing of sugar, tires, gas, tea, and coffee, a big turnout of visitors was expected in the coastal towns that summer. It was a week before the season would be in full swing, and the golf and surf clubs were getting ready to open. Soon the beach Cullen was patrolling would be crowded with vacationers staking their claims on the sand with colorful towels and umbrellas. With so many summer travelers expected, the Long Island Rail Road had just announced that it was providing additional service for the three-hour train trip from Penn Station in Manhattan to Amagansett.

But tonight, as Cullen walked through the haze, there was no one in sight. He continued to pound the sand. Cullen was about ten minutes into the job and less than a half mile from the Coast Guard station when he was startled to attention. He thought he could see dark objects in the water. He walked a little farther, then clicked on his flashlight. He quickly turned it off. He still couldn't make out what it was, so he walked a little nearer before he stopped dead in his tracks.

The dark objects were three men. They were standing in knee-deep water.

"Who are you?" Cullen shouted to the men as he shined his flashlight on them.

One of the men started walking toward him, asking, "Coast Guard?"

Cullen noticed that the man was wearing gray pants and a brown fedora hat. The brim of the hat made it difficult to see the man's face. "Yes, sir," Cullen replied.

"We are a couple of fishermen from Southampton," the man said.

"What's the trouble?" Cullen asked. He knew that it wasn't unusual for local fishermen to be out at all hours of the day and night.

The man told Cullen that their boat had run ashore.

"We left Southampton to go down to Montauk Point and we got lost and landed here."

"What are you going to do about it?" Cullen asked.

"We will stay here until sunrise," the man said. "And then we will be all right."

Sunrise was four hours away, so Cullen suggested that they come back to the Coast Guard station with him. The man hesitated, then said, "All right."

They had walked a few steps when the man suddenly stopped.

"I am not going with you," he said.

"Why?"

The man told Cullen that he didn't have any papers of identification or a fishing permit. Cullen urged him to come along anyway, but the man refused. Cullen reached out to grab his arm.

"Now, wait a minute," the man said. "You don't know what this is all about."

"No."

"How old are you?" the man asked.

"Twenty-one."

"Do you have a father?"

Cullen was feeling very uneasy but replied, "Yes."

"And a mother?"

"Yes."

"Well," the man said. "I wouldn't want to have to kill you."

The first phase of Hitler's secret attack on America, code name Operation Pastorius, had begun.

PART ONE

ONE

The Making of a Saboteur

Chapter 1

THE MASTERMINDS

Seven months earlier, November 1941
Berlin, Germany

George Dasch was dissatisfied with his job. But this was nothing new. He'd never been satisfied with any job he'd held. Even so, in Nazi Germany, his current job was considered cushy. And Dasch knew that was nothing to complain about.

He had to admit that the work was very interesting and the pay was good. Plus, there were extra food rations, cigarettes, and other luxuries that weren't available to just anyone. He also appreciated that he wasn't in any danger of being drafted into the German Army.

Dasch was an expert on all things American, which was a highly valuable skill set in Nazi Germany. He worked in a listening post as an *erfasser*, or a radio monitor. His job was to listen to American radio newscasts and translate them from English to German. But having returned to Germany after spending nearly twenty

3

years living in the United States, his command of the German language wasn't very good.

In fact, he had trouble speaking his native language. He could remember only the local dialect of his home-town of Speyer. And he could express himself only in the simplest of words, like a child. But he had no prob-lem expressing himself in English.

Dasch was a real talker, enjoying the sound of his voice and peppering his conversations with American slang and idioms, such as "scram" and "sight for sore eyes." He'd worked hard to learn English, and he spoke it with just a hint of an accent. When Dasch first started working as a radio monitor, he was worried that his rusty German was going to get him fired. But, to his sur-prise, after three weeks on the job, he was asked to take the final oath of secrecy. His cushy job was secure.

Even so, he was dissatisfied. George Dasch was thirty-eight years old and wanted to do something more, something bigger. After all, it's why he'd left his American wife behind and made the long voyage home to Nazi Germany. Dasch wanted to use his under-appreciated intelligence and find success, to make his mark on the world. Something he'd tried but failed to do in the past.

For the nearly two decades that he had lived in America, Dasch worked mostly as a waiter. He was paid well because he was good at his job. But his earnings were dependent on tips from the customers he served. And Dasch felt that the tipping system was degrading. Plus, the work was not intellectually challenging to him.

Dasch believed the job was beneath him, so he never told his mother that he worked as a waiter in America. But when she came to visit him for the first and only time, in June 1939, he couldn't hide it from her any longer. Just as he suspected, she was very disappointed in him.

"Aren't you tired of being a waiter?" she said then. "Your father and I spent our hard-earned money to give you an education, better than any of the other children, and look what you're doing now. I'm ashamed to go home and tell anyone about it."

She urged him to come back to Germany to find a more impressive job. She praised Hitler and his Nazi regime, to his surprise, and spoke persuasively about the improved living conditions and happiness of the German people. "Germany isn't the way you remember . . . We don't have unemployment any more.

Everyone is working, there's lots of building and the people are happy . . . Just keep out of politics, mind strictly your own business, and everything will be all right," she said.

Dasch felt guilty. He was one of thirteen children in his family. Throughout his childhood in the medieval city of Speyer on the Rhine, his parents had struggled to make ends meet on his father's wages as a carpenter. But his mother, whom Dasch described as a "battle axe," had always managed to somehow provide food, clothing, an education, and a home.

His shame cut deep. This wasn't the first time his mother had been disappointed in him. When he was thirteen, his parents had paid to send him to a Catholic convent so he could enter the priesthood. But a year later, when Germany was in the throes of World War I, fourteen-year-old Dasch volunteered to work as a clerk in the German Army. Three years later, Dasch went back to school, but he soon changed his mind about becoming a priest and quit. His mother felt like he had thrown an opportunity away. And Dasch quickly found himself unemployed, like many Germans after their defeat in World War I.

Unemployment wasn't all that was ailing the

German population. To make peace, the German government agreed to sign the Treaty of Versailles in June 1919. This angered and humiliated many Germans and, most notably, Adolf Hitler. Hitler had been a soldier in the war and had been wounded. He and many others believed that the German government ended the war too early and was "stabbing" the German people in the back.

By signing the treaty, Germany had accepted the blame for starting World War I and agreed to pay billions of dollars in reparations to other countries. Valuable German territory was also taken away as part of the treaty, causing the loss of industrial and agricultural income. And to hinder Germany from starting another war, the treaty reduced their armed forces, which caused more jobs to be lost. Soon, there were food

Adolf Hitler.

shortages, and inflation made their money so worthless that people began burning it for fuel. The middle class fell into poverty, and people became so desperate that the crime rate went up.

While the German economy was in a tailspin toward disaster, the Roaring Twenties were in full swing in America. The stock market was going up and up, and Americans were living big. So, like many Germans at the time, nineteen-year-old Dasch came to America in search of better opportunities. He wanted to be a success and to make his mother proud.

But he didn't have enough money to buy a ticket for passage, so Dasch snuck onto a ship and sailed to America as a stowaway. Even though he entered the country illegally, he was soon hired as a dishwasher in a restaurant. Dasch quickly learned the restaurant business and sought a job as a waiter with the goal of improving his English. Throughout the years, Dasch held various waiter jobs, working at very expensive restaurants and luxury resorts in New York City and Long Island. But in the next decade, the stock market crashed in 1929 and America suffered through the Great Depression. By the time his mother visited in 1939, Dasch felt he had nothing to show for his effort.

He wasn't even an American citizen, although he had passed all the examinations, paid the fees, and just needed to sign the final papers and be sworn in. But when Hitler invaded Poland on September 1, 1939, and launched the start of World War II, Dasch decided his duty was to his native country. He believed that if he didn't return to Germany, he would be considered "unpatriotic" and a "slacker." He didn't want to be a "rat" and renounce his German citizenship in a time of war. Plus, his mother, whose opinion he highly valued, had persuaded him that Hitler was leading Germany down the right path. She convinced him that he wasn't a success in America but there was a chance he would be one in Germany.

At the time, the Nazi regime was encouraging Germans living outside of the country to return to their homeland. The government was even paying for their passage back. But they weren't letting just anyone return. They wanted men with specific skill sets and experience to help Hitler win the war. They also wanted Nazis. This last piece was a problem for Dasch.

He wasn't a member of the Nazi Party, or any political party. Although people who knew Dasch would call him a communist, he considered himself a socialist, like his mother. He strongly supported more rights and equality for the working class, such as better wages and the right to join labor unions. In fact, Dasch had taken it upon himself to organize a union for waiters in New York City.

But in Hitler's Germany, labor unions were outlawed, and neither communism nor socialism was tolerated even though the Nazi Party's full name was the National Socialist German Workers' Party. Many German socialists were arrested and imprisoned. At the same time, the Nazi Party considered democracy even worse, and was vehemently opposed to it.

When Hitler was appointed the chancellor of Germany six years before Dasch decided to return, on January 30, 1933, it marked the end of democracy for the country and the beginning of nationalism. By invoking a state of emergency, Hitler was able to suspend Germany's constitution. This gave Hitler all the power, and he could issue new laws without consulting anyone.

Dasch watched from afar as Hitler established a one-party state and banned all other political parties. This eliminated elections and the people's right to vote. But the German people were desperate for change, and many believed Hitler's message that he was their savior.

Hitler was a charismatic and hypnotic speaker. He spoke passionately, using simple and clear language, and told the people what they wanted to hear. The Nazis were going to solve all their problems, which at first, Dasch did not believe.

In the beginning, Hitler was vague about the Nazi Party's policies. He wanted to reach a wide range of people. He promised to abolish the Treaty of Versailles, calling it "unfair punishment." Many Germans agreed with him. He also promised more jobs, which appealed to the unemployed working class—and would resonate strongly with Dasch.

From what Dasch was told by his mother, Hitler delivered on these promises. But the increase in employment wasn't what it seemed. The Nazi Party used propaganda, which was a powerful weapon, allowing them to twist the truth or outright lie to support their agenda. They also used censorship to silence any opposition to their message.

So, while the Nazis did increase the number of new jobs by building and repairing roads, railways, and houses as well as building up their military, they also took employment away from other Germans. Many women and Jews were fired from their jobs, but the Nazis did not count them as unemployed. This made it seem like unemployment had decreased. And, perhaps more important for Hitler, it made him look like he was saving Germany, compelling many Germans, including Dasch, to return.

To maintain his power, Hitler quickly turned Germany into a police state. He took away basic freedoms, such as the freedoms of speech, press, and assembly. The German people also lost their right to privacy, so government officials could read their mail, listen to their telephone conversations, and search their homes without needing a warrant.

Hitler controlled all aspects of their lives, including their leisure time. Teenaged boys were required to join Hitler Youth groups, where they were groomed to become Nazis.

Hitler also spread hate by promoting the belief that Germans were a superior race of humans called Aryans. Textbooks were rewritten to teach students that some races were *Untermensch*, meaning subhuman. Under Hitler's rule, this meant ridding the country of anyone who was not of pure German blood through terrorist tactics, like intimidation and savage violence. Specifically, he was targeting people of the Jewish faith, but it also included Jehovah's Witnesses, Catholic priests, anyone with a physical or mental disability, Roma, black people, homosexuals, prostitutes, alcoholics, pacifists, vagrants, and criminals.

To enforce his absolute authority as the leader, or Führer, of the Nazi regime, Hitler created his own private army composed of fanatical Nazis called the Schutzstaffel, or SS. They were his execution squad, and they eliminated any of his enemies.

Anyone who wasn't a Nazi, like George Dasch, was targeted as an enemy of the state. And an enemy of the state was an enemy of Adolf Hitler.

So, when Dasch went to the German Consulate in New York City to inquire about returning to Germany, they

George Dasch was one of the estimated 20,000 people who attended the German American Bund Rally at Madison Square Garden on February 20, 1939.

weren't receptive to him at first. Dasch was "politically unreliable" because he wasn't a Nazi. He wasn't even a member of the German American Bund, a Hitler-endorsed organization comprising an estimated 25,000 dues-paying Germans living in America. The Bund fully supported the Nazis' principles that were rooted in anti-Semitism, anti-communist sentiments, and the demand that the United States remain neutral in the war. The German American Bund produced propaganda to further its cause, publishing magazines and brochures, organizing demonstrations, and running Hitler Youth–like camps.

But Dasch was dead set on returning to Germany. It was his second chance for success. So he lied. He falsified his political creed to the German Consulate.

He also didn't mention that he was a waiter. Instead, Dasch lied again, telling them he was a salesman for an importer and exporter of goods that had secretly benefited Nazi Germany. The German officials didn't check to see if it was true. But it still took many, many months of persuasive pestering before Dasch received a new German passport and a ticket back to Germany.

But once he received them, there was no time to spare. On the same day that he was granted permission

The Nazi Party recruited children with mandatory membership in Hitler Youth groups. Here the recruits are singing the praises of Hitler.

to return to Germany, Dasch quickly packed. Without saying goodbye, he left his American wife, Rose Marie, who was in the hospital recovering from surgery. Once she was well and Dasch was repatriated, Rose Marie knew that she was to follow him.

Over the next several days, Dasch traveled by bus across America to San Francisco. Once there, he boarded a ship full of Nazi-supporting passengers heading back to Germany by way of Japan.

When Dasch arrived in Germany seven weeks later, in June 1941, he and his fellow returning German citizens were taken to a hotel where they were welcomed and hailed as heroes for returning to their Fatherland. Dasch spent the next day filling out paperwork. When he was asked, "Why did you return to Germany?" he answered, "To participate politically."

He also rehearsed in his head the lie about his occupation. He told the German officials that he was an importer in America, hinting that Germany somehow benefited from his work. They had no way of checking out his story. But Dasch knew that any little slipup, such as revealing that he had been a member of a labor union, would mean "curtains."

After telling them his life story, he was given some money so he could travel to his family in Speyer. When he arrived home, his family was shocked but happy to see him. But later, his mother told him he had made a mistake coming back despite what she'd told him two years ago.

"Things are different now," she said. "We have a war. You shouldn't have done it."

Dasch tried to push aside any misgivings, but it was difficult to expel them from his mind in Nazi Germany.

Even so, he immediately tried to find a job, but, to his frustration, it wasn't easy for him. He quickly realized that in order to get hired or promoted, you needed to know someone in the Nazi Party.

But then he remembered meeting his wife's cousin and her cousin's husband, Reinhold Barth. When they met, the bespectacled Barth was a quiet man who had worked for the Long Island Rail Road. Dasch remembered Barth as "an idealistic Nazi," and he had returned to Germany a couple of years ago. So Dasch contacted him.

They met and talked a lot. Dasch convinced him that he had returned to help Germany win the war. "I gave him a lot of talk about my duty, my desire to fight, and my willingness to die for my country . . . and I confided in him that I was willing to do something big," Dasch later recounted.

Through Barth's recommendation, Dasch soon found himself sitting in the office of a baby-faced man with thinning blond hair and a big belly. There was a gold Nazi Party emblem near his heart on his uniform that signaled he was a long-standing member of the Nazi Party. The man's name was Walter Kappe.

Kappe had lived in America for a dozen years, where he was referred to as "the No. 1 Nazi in the

United States" before he was deported in 1939. He had worked as a journalist for a German-language newspaper in Chicago. He was an energetic but unscrupulous reporter, willing to take bribes to slant stories. Kappe was finally fired when he wrote an anti-Semitic article about a Jewish businessman. So Kappe moved to Cincinnati and worked as the press and propaganda chief of the German American Bund. When he returned to Germany after being deported, he was made a lieutenant and worked in the Abwehr, the Intelligence Department of the German Army. Like Dasch, he was ambitious, yearning for more power and success.

That wasn't all he and Dasch had in common. Kappe was also long-winded. And he had some more questions for Dasch about his work, how long he'd lived in America, and his politics. Dasch struggled to reply in German, so Kappe switched to English and used a fake British accent to try to hide his harsh German accent.

Replying in near-perfect English, Dasch informed Kappe that he wanted to join the German Army and be a soldier. Kappe told him he was crazy and wouldn't last two weeks in the military because he was too used to having his freedom. And there was also another reason.

"A man with your knowledge of English and of America in general does not come to Germany every day, and would be wanted in almost every department of the German government," said Kappe.

He had something else in mind for Dasch. Kappe asked Dasch if he wanted to work for either the German foreign office or some other endeavor. The "other endeavor" sounded vague, so Dasch asked what kind of work he would be doing in the foreign office. Kappe described a radio monitor position at the listening post. Dasch told him he was willing to do that, and one phone call later, Dasch had a job.

But Walter Kappe already had Dasch in mind for something else—something bigger and better. It was the "other endeavor" that Kappe was organizing. He worked in the sabotage division of the Abwehr, and he had hatched a plot against America.

Although Hitler was at the height of his power, having conquered Czechoslovakia, Austria, Poland, the Balkans, the Netherlands, France, and parts of Russia, he remained worried about the United States. It wasn't America's military strength that he worried about. He didn't think much of the American soldiers. Hitler had fought against them in World War I and said, "I'll never believe that an American soldier can fight like a hero." But he was worried about America's industrial strength.

America's factories efficiently mass-produced military weapons, planes, tanks, cars, and other machinery with fewer workers and at a lower cost. Hitler believed that the country with the most industrial strength would win the war. He needed to destroy America's infrastructure by blowing up factories, power plants, water supply systems, and bridges.

The problem was that Hitler didn't have any Nazi saboteurs in America anymore. Recently, a Nazi spy in America, William Sebold, had gone to the FBI and blown the cover off Hitler's existing spy ring, destroying it. While the FBI and America viewed Sebold as a hero, the Germans branded him a traitor. Without a network of secret agents in America, Hitler needed to build a new one.

So Walter Kappe had come up with the idea to send Germans who had already lived in the United States back to infiltrate the country and establish a new spy network. He was put in charge of organizing and recruiting candidates. Kappe had been impressed with Dasch, and when he heard Dasch was dissatisfied with his job at the listening post less than six months later, he called him back to his office in November 1941. He had Dasch sign an oath of secrecy before he revealed a few facts.

First, Kappe hinted that something was soon going to happen that would expedite a plan he and his office had been working on for some time. Then he said:

"George, how would you like to go back to America?"

"What do you mean, America?" Dasch replied. "That's a peaceful country, isn't it?"

"Yes, it is a neutral country," Kappe continued. "But they are indirect enemies today because they are helping our enemies with their supplies. Therefore, it is time for us to attack them. We wish to attack the American industries by industrial sabotage. How much do you know about that? Would you mind trying to put together your ideas and write them in English and bring them to me?"

Dasch didn't hesitate. "Yes, I will do that."

He went home and started writing down his ideas right away, pointing out which American industries could be easily destroyed with high explosives. He also described how a Nazi saboteur should act while in America, so he would blend in and not draw attention to himself and the mission. Dasch tried to think of every possible idea, wanting to prove his worth and earn Kappe's respect. After a week, he carried the five-page memorandum to Kappe's office and delivered it himself.

A few days after Pearl Harbor was bombed, in December 1941, Dasch found himself back in Kappe's office. Now that the United States had entered the war, Hitler wanted fast action on Kappe's plan.

An unnamed man with an Irish accent was also in Kappe's office when Dasch arrived. He asked Dasch, "Have you ever been on board of a sailing vessel? Are you a good sailor?"

"On the contrary," Dasch replied. He'd sailed the seven seas and got very seasick every time.

Despite Dasch's weak stomach, the unnamed man told Kappe that Dasch was a wonderful prospect because he looked and acted like an American, so no one would ever suspect Dasch of working for the Germans. Kappe told Dasch to be patient. He was doing everything he could to make his plan happen quickly. Dasch felt nervous excitement at the thought of being considered for such an important mission.

On January 10, 1942, Dasch was told to meet with Kappe. He went to Kappe's office in the headquarters of the German High Command, where Dasch met a man named Captain Astor.

Astor had spent time in America and had studied Dasch's five-page memo. He was also impressed with Dasch, and told him to meet him the next day at the following address: Schriftleitung Der Kaukasus, 6 Rankenstrasse, Berlin, on the fourth floor.

Schriftleitung Der Kaukasus translated in English meant the editorial office of the *Caucasus* newspaper. But that wasn't what it really was. It was just a front for the secret office of Walter Kappe.

It was time for Dasch to help lay the groundwork and recruit some other men. Finally, Dasch was about to be treated as a very important person. He was going to be the leader of a team of Nazi saboteurs.

Dasch felt shock and excitement. His heart was thumping so hard he couldn't think straight. But he knew there was no backing out now. He was going to go through with it.

And if the mission was a success, Dasch was promised a powerful position in the German government. Finally, something bigger and better.

Chapter 2

RECRUITING A SABOTEUR

March 1942
(Three months after the
Japanese bombed Pearl Harbor)

Herbert Haupt liked to wear stylish and flashy clothes, but today they were hidden underneath an overcoat. Even so, the big silver ring on his finger was shiny and bright. Although Haupt was a dapper dresser, he was a big spender and flat broke. So he'd had to borrow money from his relatives to buy a train ticket from the seaport town of Stettin to the bustling big city of Berlin. It was almost a hundred-mile journey, but there was the promise of a potential job in Berlin.

When Haupt arrived about two hours later and stepped off the train, he was in the commercial district. As he walked down a tree-lined street, the only other young, physically fit men like himself were Nazis, and all were wearing the swastika.

The office where Haupt was expected wasn't far from the famous Berlin Zoo. The zoo was a prestigious social hot spot for many German people, but Jews hadn't been allowed in the park since 1939. Socializing with Jews was strictly forbidden for all German citizens.

As Haupt passed by the store windows, he saw their displays of elegant clothing. Haupt didn't have many warm clothes to wear. But inside the stores, the racks were nearly bare. And the window displays were just for show. Clothes were rationed. Strict guidelines were enforced, and new shoes were nearly impossible to obtain. So even if Haupt had money to spend, there was nothing worth buying anyway, unless he wanted to wear clothes made of cellulose "wool." The thin texture of cellulose wool felt rigid and rough. It wasn't anything Haupt would choose to wear.

As he continued walking, it was difficult not to notice the signs prominently displayed in the store windows, declaring, NO JEWS PERMITTED. In addition to the signs, it was hard to miss the anti-Jewish posters littering the city and falsely declaring: "THE JEWS WANTED THIS WAR. THEY SHALL HAVE IT. THEY ALL MUST DIE. THAT IS THE DUTY OF EVERY GERMAN."

Prisoners in a concentration camp.

In January, Hitler's plan for a "final solution" was underway. His plan was to physically annihilate all the Jews in Europe. Jewish men, women, and children were now required to wear a yellow star on their clothes. And Jews were being rounded up and separated from the rest of the population. They were being forced to live in crowded ghettos, where many would die from disease and starvation. Those who managed to survive the unbearable living conditions would later be sent to concentration camps and killing centers.

But Haupt wasn't thinking about Hitler's final solution plan as he made his way down the street. He was hoping to fix all his problems. That was why he was going to a meeting at Schriftleitung Der Kaukasus. It was the second time Walter Kappe had summoned him. The first time he had met with Kappe, Haupt was under the impression that he could earn some money for a magazine article about his life.

By now Haupt suspected that Kappe wasn't really in the magazine business or interviewing him for an article. But when he was ushered into the fancy reception area to wait for his appointment, he was unaware that there was a hidden microphone and spy hole nearby so that Kappe could monitor him. Trust was a luxury that no one could afford in Nazi Germany. And Haupt had been learning that the hard way.

Haupt was shown into Kappe's office for his appointment. During this second interview, Kappe offered him a job. Haupt wasn't told any details about the job, just that it was a secret mission that involved going home to America. It soon became very clear to Haupt that he shouldn't turn down the offer.

"Do you know that your mother's brother is in a concentration camp?" Kappe asked Haupt.

"Yes."

"Have you noticed that you can't get a job, and the Gestapo and police are bothering you?" Kappe continued. "The only thing left for you to do is return to the United States."

Haupt agreed. Kappe was giving him little choice, and besides, he desperately wanted to go home and resume his "lively" life. That was something he couldn't have in Nazi Germany.

Before the offer was finalized, Haupt was ushered into another office down the hall, where a thin man with a streak of gray hair introduced himself. He told Haupt his name was George Davis. That wasn't his real name. His real name was George Dasch, and he had a few more questions for Haupt.

Part of Dasch's job was to go through the files of prospective saboteurs and learn their personal histories. Dasch studied Haupt closely. It was his responsibility to determine each candidate's "fitness" based on how fluent they were in English and how well they knew America and its culture. Dasch wasn't impressed with many of them, calling them "a bunch of nitwits." He particularly didn't like it when the candidate was only interested in his own personal advancement or just wanted to get out of Germany.

Dasch didn't want to make a mistake. He knew that Kappe was not only relying on him but, perhaps more important, needed him.

Although Kappe had made himself valuable to the German High Command by positioning himself as an expert on America, Dasch believed that Kappe's knowledge was limited in scope to the German American conflict. In Dasch's opinion, he, not Kappe, was the expert on all things American.

If Kappe needed to give his opinion on anything, Dasch noticed that Kappe asked him for all kinds of information. Dasch figured Kappe probably felt more assured if he knew what Dasch thought about matters concerning America and the mission.

Although Dasch thought he'd been "given the privilege of offering my opinion upon the ability of each man who was to accompany us on the mission," he also felt a lot of pressure with his new job as the lead saboteur. And the strain of helping to plan the mission, which involved outlining what they were going to do after arriving, had made him very tense. He had always been a nervous and impulsive person, but lately his emotions were almost out of control.

"Love and hate and a little bit of courage and lots of fear would all rush over me at once and grip my throat and tighten me up," Dasch described. "In a few seconds I would break out in tears."

But he managed to maintain his composure in public. His training as a waiter had polished his public persona. Dasch possessed good manners and spoke eloquently, seemingly unaware that he often touched his nose or forehead with his index finger when he talked.

After the introductions, Dasch asked Haupt to give him more details of his life.

In June 1941, six months before America entered World War II and as Hitler was launching his attack on Russia, twenty-one-year-old Herbie Haupt and his friend, eighteen-year-old Wolfgang Wergin, loaded up the car in their hometown of Chicago and took off for Mexico City. It was supposed to be the adventure of a lifetime. And it was. But nothing had turned out as either of them expected. They never intended to end up in Nazi Germany.

Their plan was to find jobs in Mexico, earn some money, then continue their travels toward South America, finding more work along the way. They didn't know, until they arrived, that they needed work permits, which they couldn't obtain. Even so, the bad news didn't ruin their trip. Haupt and Wergin had grown up in "strait-laced families," and this was the greatest adventure of their lives.

Although Haupt and Wergin were American citizens, they were both born in Germany. Not long after the end of World War I, when Haupt was five years old, his family moved to Chicago's North Side. They settled into a neighborhood where other German immigrants lived.

Haupt's father, Hans, was a bricklayer and had found work as a contractor and painter. Although they had not been back to Germany, Hans had instilled in his only child a fervent passion for the Fatherland.

"It was unusual for kids, even in our German neighborhood, to be so in love with Germany," said one of Haupt's friends. "I would call him fanatical."

When Haupt was a teenager, he became a member of the German American Bund. He participated enthusiastically in their demonstrations, wearing a uniform with the swastika emblem and marching with his knees unbent in the goose-step style, like the Nazis that he fully supported.

Haupt was outspoken about his beliefs. Once, at a dance party, he began talking about how Germany was superior to the United States. Haupt's best friend, Larry Jordan, responded to the lecture with his fist. He punched Haupt squarely in the nose, ending the conversation but not their friendship.

All the same, Haupt's main interest in life was having a good time, which was what he and Wergin planned on doing in Mexico City. After all, that's why they'd left their jobs at Simpson Optical Company. Haupt had been an apprentice optician since dropping out of high school a few years ago. He had worked on government orders, camera lenses, and microscopes, earning twenty-five dollars a week. Haupt lived with his parents, so he handed his paycheck over to his father. But both Haupt and Wergin had brought eighty dollars along to fund their adventure. So they went out, met some girls, and had fun, night after night.

But not long after arriving in Mexico, they were nearly out of money. The final straw was when the sisters they were dating brought their extended family along on an outing, and Haupt and Wergin learned they were obliged to buy everyone's drinks. Luckily, they managed to sneak out without paying. Without money to line their pockets, their fun was over.

Even though they didn't want to, it was time to return to Chicago. But there was one major sticking point: They didn't have enough money to buy gas for the car ride home.

Ever resourceful, Wergin sold his Chevy, and they bought train tickets to Nuevo Laredo, a town bordering Texas. But the Mexican authorities wouldn't let them cross the border until they paid the tax on their recently sold car. They didn't have enough money, and Haupt wasn't about to ask his parents to send him some.

"My mother had just undergone a very serious surgery, my car was not paid for, the doctor had to be paid, and my father was occasionally sick," Haupt said. "In fact, I was going to send them money if I was working, not try to get money out of them."

There were other reasons too. He was keeping a secret from his parents. He was worried that when they found out, they would be ashamed of him. But Haupt didn't want to think about that. He also didn't want to have to register for the draft. If America went to war with Germany, Haupt didn't want to fight against his Fatherland. So he was content to stay stuck in Mexico for now. Despite being low on funds, it didn't dampen their spirits. To them, the hairier the situation became, the more exciting it was.

And things were about to get even hairier.

They went back to Mexico City, where their new friends told them to go to Manzanillo, a port town situated on the Pacific Ocean with beautiful beaches. In Manzanillo, they might find a freighter headed to California, and they could probably hitch a ride. At the time, it sounded like a good idea.

But a few days later, when Haupt was eating at a restaurant, he met a German agent named Hans Sass, who also used the aliases Paul Smith and Dr. Reichal. After their conversation, Haupt's plans dramatically changed.

Sass took Haupt to the German Embassy and introduced him to an official. Haupt told the official that he was a German boy who needed help or a job, and was there anything he could do for him?

He offered Haupt a job in a monastery in Japan. But he would have to pay them back for the trip. In other words, Haupt would be obligated to the German government.

Haupt still wasn't ready to go back home. He feared his parents' disappointment in him. It wasn't because he failed to make things work in Mexico. He was worried about what they would think about his girlfriend, Gerda, whom he left behind in Chicago, and the secret he was keeping about her. Even though he'd been dating her for two years, his parents didn't approve of her. And he hadn't told them that Gerda was five months pregnant with his child. Haupt didn't want to have to marry her, which was what his parents and her parents would expect.

"My plans were to, first of all, stay away from the girl until everything died down," Haupt said.

So he told his friend Wergin there was a freighter they could board that was heading to Japan with a stop in California. Wergin planned to get off in California, but a couple of days into the journey, he found out the freighter was heading directly to Japan. It never crossed his mind that his friend may have lied to him about their destination. Wergin never would have boarded the ship if he'd known. But he wouldn't learn the truth until a long time after the fact.

One month later, on August 24, 1941, they arrived in Japan and went to the monastery, which was run by

German monks, to start their jobs on the farm. But it was not what Haupt and Wergin expected. The monastery was a labor camp.

"The conditions there were so bad, and they had so many sick and everything, that my friend and I decided we wouldn't work there," Haupt said.

They went back to Tokyo and asked the German Consulate for different jobs. They were offered one option: to be sailors. They took it. And a few weeks later they found themselves on an unnamed ship on their way to an unknown destination. After they passed the Gilbert Islands, they learned they were going to Germany.

When they arrived months later, in December 1941, America and Germany were at war. Even though Haupt had earned two medals on his voyage for spotting a British naval blockade and warning the ship to run past it safely, Haupt and Wergin weren't allowed to leave the freighter. Although the German Consulate issued them German passports, they were American citizens— enemies of Hitler and the Nazi regime.

The Gestapo, Hitler's brutal Secret State Police, were suspicious of Haupt and Wergin. Their story about Mexico seemed unbelievable, and they thought the two were American spies. After three days of intense questioning, Haupt and Wergin were finally released to their remaining relatives in Germany. But the Gestapo would not give Haupt a work permit. In fact, they harassed him several times a week. That was something the fun-loving Haupt was worried about.

The Gestapo answered to no one. Any crime they committed was not investigated, giving them the power to arrest, harm, imprison, and kill without consequence. People routinely disappeared. But neighbors, friends, and family knew better than to protest, knowing and fearing that they would be next. Upon arriving in Germany, Haupt had learned that two of his uncles had been sent to a concentration camp. This was not the welcome that Haupt had expected from his Fatherland.

He was being hounded by the Gestapo, the police, and the army. They made it clear that they didn't trust him.

So when he received a letter from Walter Kappe telling him that Hans Sass, the man he had met in Mexico City at a restaurant, had recommended him for a job, Haupt jumped at the chance to earn some money. With no other prospects in sight, and the Gestapo on his back, what choice did he have? So he borrowed money from his relatives to buy a train ticket to Berlin. He hoped his luck was about to change. And it was. But not for the better.

After learning Haupt's life story, Dasch thought that Haupt ending up in Germany was more like the *mis*adventure of a lifetime. "I felt his return to Germany had been something of a boyish lark and he had ended up trapped . . . still there was something serious about him."

Dasch noted that Haupt's English was better than his German. He recognized the American slang Haupt used when he spoke. Dasch had also noticed that when Haupt removed his overcoat, he was wearing nice clothes.

Dasch detected a shrewdness in Haupt, and street smarts. He described Haupt as a "drugstore cowboy," which was slang for a young man who hangs out on street corners or drugstores. Although Haupt courted danger, he managed to dodge any fatal consequences— a useful and valuable skill for a saboteur. Dasch thought Haupt was a good candidate for the mission.

Per Kappe's instructions, Dasch sent Haupt back to his relatives in Stettin, informing him to come back after Easter with his belongings.

"Tell them that you have been in Berlin to investigate . . . possibilities of getting into the Flying Service," Dasch told him. He also advised Haupt to keep quiet. "Say nothing about what you have heard."

But this was one secret Haupt couldn't keep to himself. He met with his friend Wolfgang Wergin at his grandmother's home one more time. Wergin already had some idea about Haupt's situation because Haupt had recommended Wergin as a potential candidate to Kappe.

"Wergin will be held in Germany," Kappe had said.

Haupt understood what Kappe meant. Wergin was Kappe's collateral, so Haupt wouldn't "double-cross this whole thing."

Wergin wasn't interested in going on a secret mission anyway. He thought it sounded "idiotic" and tried to talk Haupt out of going through with it. He'd seen plenty of gangster movies, and the FBI always caught the bad guys.

"You can't get away from the FBI," Wergin warned him. "They're going to catch you and stick you in jail." The idea that his friend could get executed never entered Wergin's mind. Otherwise, he would have argued that point too.

"I'm just going to go and disappear," Haupt said. He felt trapped, and thought he could solve his problems by simply running away.

Wergin was surprised when Haupt was overcome with emotion and began to cry. He'd always looked to Haupt for guidance, and tonight, their roles were reversed. Wergin continued to try to talk his friend out of going on the mission. But Haupt had made his decision. He just wanted to go home. He would worry about the consequences later.

Chapter 3

HITLER'S SCHOOL FOR SABOTEURS

April 1942
Quenz Lake, Brandenburg, Germany
35 miles from Berlin

F rom the gated entrance, it looked like a working farm. And it was. There was a barn where the cows and pigs were kept, and there was a greenhouse filled with blooming flowers and growing vegetables. The farmer, along with his wife and children, lived in a one-story stone house on the farm. Nearby, their ducks waddled about and their chickens pecked the ground, searching for bits of food. At first glance, it looked like an idyllic pastoral setting—except there were guards in Nazi uniforms on the premises and a stone wall with a barbed-wire fence surrounding it. Signs were clearly posted on the fence, blaring, KEEP OUT! UNDER THE SEVERE PUNISHMENT OF THE LAW. When night fell, the manager of the property patrolled the grounds with three big German shepherds. He was armed with a machine gun.

Just beyond the iron-gated entrance, about a football field's length away, stood a large two-story manor house surrounded by a park and garden. The country estate was nestled between the shores of Quenz Lake and the pine-scented Brandenburg Forest. But even the forest wasn't as idyllic as it seemed. Among the evergreen pine trees, Nazis had stealthily planted larch trees. In the autumn, only the larch trees changed color, revealing a golden-yellow swastika in the center of the swath of green.

The country estate on Quenz Lake was so picturesque that one saboteur-in-training thought, at first, he was at a country club. The Nazi regime had seized the estate from a wealthy Jewish shoe manufacturer. Now it was Hitler's school for sabotage.

Inside the two-story manor house there were twelve rooms, some of which had been converted to better serve the school. On the ground floor, there was a front office, a kitchen, two dining rooms, and a reading room that was well stocked with American newspapers and magazines, such as the *New York Times*, *Life*, and the *Saturday Evening Post*.

Next to the reading room, near the center of the house, there were six rooms where the saboteurs slept. They also had access to a living room, and they ate together at four tables in one of the dining rooms. The Nazi officers and instructors ate in their own dining room and slept upstairs, where there were several more rooms.

Near the manor house, there was another two-story building where there were bathrooms. Upstairs, there was a science laboratory fully equipped with glass beakers, test tubes, and a variety of scales, batteries, and chemicals. Next to it was a classroom where George Dasch and several other men were sitting down on hard benches. They'd been given heavy military uniforms to wear that once belonged to the now-defeated Polish army. But the uniforms had been dyed blue.

Dasch was familiar with most of the men in the class from reading their files and questioning them. One of them he had met on his voyage back to Germany. And Dasch had told Kappe that he was "quite sure he was the right type of man" for the mission. That man was introduced as William Thomas. But that wasn't his real name. The men were instructed not to reveal their real names to one another and to choose an alias. William Thomas's real name was Werner Thiel.

Thiel had lived in America for fourteen years and worked as a toolmaker for automobile factories. His work experience gave him an edge for sabotaging factories. He was also a loyal Nazi, having been a member of the German American Bund. It was through the Bund that Thiel had also known Kappe while living in America. A year after returning to Germany, he ran into Kappe and Dasch at a social gathering for Germans who had lived in America.

Dasch asked Thiel if he would like to go back to the United States.

"Why?" Thiel asked.

"For the good of the Fatherland," was all Dasch would say.

That was enough for Thiel.

Not long after, Thiel received a letter in the mail instructing him to go to Schriftleitung Der Kaukasus. He went and met Dasch and Kappe in the secret office. They talked about how nice it would be for those who were familiar with the United States to go back and do something for the Fatherland. Thiel agreed, then asked:

"What's this all about?"

Kappe wouldn't say. But he did tell Thiel that he would "have to go some place and take a special course."

Thiel and the other recruits found out the details on Monday, April 13, 1942. It was ten o'clock in the morning, and the first day of class. The man in charge of the school for sabotage, Walter Kappe, was giving a lecture to his handpicked students.

Kappe welcomed them and stressed that their secret mission was just as important as any big battle on the front lines. He informed them that they were going to be schooled in the use of explosives and incendiaries. The first goal of the mission was to sabotage America's light-metals industry to stop the manufacturing of products needed in war, especially airplanes.

The sabotage targets had been carefully selected to pinpoint areas that, when attacked, would create bottlenecks in the American war industry. In fact, some of the factories on their target list had no guards of any type even though what they manufactured was essential. And the Nazis had the complete plans (drawings and photographs) of the Aluminum Company of America (Alcoa) plant in Tennessee. Incredibly, the same engineers and chemists who explained the inner workings of the Alcoa plant to the saboteurs had supervised the construction of them.

The sabotage plan was simple. They were to blow

up the steel towers carrying high-tension wires to the plant to cut off the power supply.

On that first day of class, Kappe also told them that the second goal of the mission was to "stir up trouble" to turn Americans against German Americans, Japanese Americans, and Italian Americans. In other words, anyone who was from a country that was part of the Axis, Germany's allies.

The saboteurs were to recruit Nazi sympathizers and supply them with dynamite, incendiaries, and small bombs. The recruits were to commit "minor sabotage of a nuisance nature," to prey on America's fear and provoke prejudice against any person possibly connected to Germany, Japan, and Italy. By inflaming feelings of bigotry and hate toward certain ethnic groups, other Americans would marginalize and stigmatize them, resulting in mutual animosity and distrust. Ultimately it would open the door to "vitalize a real Fifth Column movement in the United States."

To vitalize a fifth column, they would create a large network of Nazi sympathizers working against the United States from within the United States. Walter Kappe had come up with the idea based on how the

United States had reacted to their Japanese American citizens.

After Pearl Harbor was bombed, the U.S. government feared that anyone who was of Japanese descent living in America could not be trusted. With no supporting evidence, it was believed that Japanese Americans would act as spies and saboteurs for Japan.

eft: A war poster encouraging Americans to do their part in keeping America nited by remaining loyal to the four pillars that uphold the nation: liberty, unity, stice, and equality.

ight: A Nazi propaganda poster showing the strength and power of the fearsome

So President Franklin Roosevelt signed Executive Order 9066 on February 19, 1942. And, like the Jews in Germany, Japanese American citizens—men, women, and children—were rounded up and forced to live in internment camps with no regard for their civil rights.

Kappe had carefully researched and plotted out his plan. He knew the number of German Americans living in the United States and had compiled numerous charts, statistics, and personal information, such as their occupations and if they were Bund members. The saboteurs were instructed "to carry out small acts of terrorism," such as dropping off a suitcase packed with a bomb at a luggage depot or in a Jewish-owned store. But they were to be careful not to kill or injure anyone, because that would create feelings of indignation toward Germany. The idea was for the saboteurs themselves to blend in, but their acts of terrorism to stand out. That way, the American public would know Hitler had a long reach, igniting fear, panic, and prejudice.

With the details of the secret mission finally revealed, Kappe introduced the two main instructors. Although the saboteurs were told they could speak to one another only in English from now on, their classes were taught in German. Neither instructor was fluent in English.

A man with thin blond hair named Dr. Walter König would teach them general chemistry and how explosives worked. In addition to teaching, König worked in a laboratory in Berlin, where he was busy creating new sabotage equipment. He was "ambitious," a "fanatical Nazi," and "loyal to the regime."

The other instructor was Dr. Günther Schulz. His job was to teach them how to physically build the explosives. Unlike König, he hated the Nazi regime. Schulz had been in trouble with the Gestapo and, as a result, lost his previous job as an oil expert. He was secretly hoping for a revolution so he could take part.

Over the next three weeks, the men fell into a routine. On a typical day, the men woke up at seven o'clock for thirty minutes of physical training. Afterward, they made up their beds and ate breakfast. The food at the school was much better than what they ate as civilians. Civilians were given just enough food rations to keep them alive.

Prior to coming to sabotage school, Dasch was always "hungry like the dickens," and he made sure to carefully divvy up his bread ration and carry it with him. Dasch explained that "ordinary food tasted too good because you were hungry, just plain hungry . . . The food you ate filled you up for a moment but in an hour or so later you were hungry like a dog."

So after eating breakfast, with full stomachs, the saboteurs attended classes from nine o'clock until noon. They were taught general chemistry and had to memorize basic formulas in bomb making. The emphasis was on teaching the men how to make explosives using ordinary items from a store, such as dried peas, flour, powdered sugar, a thumbtack, a tin can, a pocket watch, bare wires, and a postcard.

Their instructors, König and Schulz, had also built sabotage equipment for the men to take with them and use in America. There was compressed but stable dynamite cleverly camouflaged with plastic and painted black so it looked like a lump of coal. The dynamite, which, unpainted, looked like yellow Play-Doh, could be dropped, cut, smashed, and even burned without exploding. There was a special detonator that was required to make it burn hot enough to cause an explosion.

The men were also given special matches. Each match was actually a pen that wrote with invisible ink.

They were taught how to make more invisible ink using things like aspirin and Ex-Lax. The invisible ink would allow them to communicate with one another in America via letters. Even if their words fell into the wrong hands, nothing about their plans would be revealed.

Following their morning class, there was an hour for lunch, and from one o'clock to two o'clock the men read American magazines and newspapers so they were familiar with current events. From two to four o'clock they were back in class, and afterward, they went to the gymnasium or sports field, where they practiced gymnastics, football, boxing, discus and hand-grenade throwing, and wrestling.

In the evenings, sometimes they learned American songs, singing Francis Scott Key's "The Star-Spangled Banner," and Stephen Foster's "Oh! Susanna" and "The Swanee River (Old Folks at Home)." There were also lectures on American speech, manners, history, and geography.

The men spent a lot of their other time working on their new identities and rehearsing their cover stories. Kappe was going to give them fake identification papers. But if they were ever questioned or arrested in America, they needed to know their new life histories inside and out so they sounded natural and, most important, believable.

As an expert on American ways, Kappe ordered Dasch to take charge and help create plausible cover stories that would stand up under intense scrutiny. Dasch worked hard to help the men create and learn their new identities, and he was proud of his efforts.

The men had been divided up into different teams, and each team was going to land in a different spot along the East Coast of America. Dasch, who was the leader of the first team, chose Long Island because he was very familiar with the area, having lived and worked there as a waiter.

The three men under his leadership were Richard Quirin, Heinrich Heinck, and Peter Burger. Quirin and Heinck had worked together at a Volkswagen factory where Kappe had held a meeting and secretly recruited them.

Richard Quirin strongly resembled George Dasch in looks, and many asked if they were brothers. But they weren't related. Quirin had proved to be intelligent, audacious, and loyal to the Nazi Party. During his time in America, Quirin had worked as a handyman, chauffeur, and mechanic. But when he returned to Nazi Germany, he worked as a toolmaker at the Volkswagen factory with Heinck.

The most distinguishing feature of Heinrich Heinck was a noticeable scar in the middle of his forehead. It was caused by an accident that had happened at his factory job. A piece of iron flew out from a machine and sliced his forehead. Heinck had lived in America for several years, working in various American factories before returning to Germany. He had previously met Walter Kappe while living in America through the German American Bund. Heinck thought that the leader of his group, Dasch, was intelligent. But Dasch and some of the other saboteurs thought Heinck was "slow witted." Even so, once Heinck finally learned something, he didn't forget it. He followed orders, as did his friend Quirin, whom he relied on. Heinck and Quirin were on the mission because they were told to be. No questions asked.

The third man on Dasch's team was Peter Burger. His file had captured Dasch's attention. Burger had recently spent seventeen months in a concentration camp. He was a long-standing member of the Nazi

Party and had been a volunteer member of the notorious storm troopers (SA), also known as "brown shirts" for the uniforms they wore.

The storm troopers were a private Nazi army feared for their aggressive brutality and violence. Burger had worked as an aide-de-camp ("confidential assistant"), reporting directly to Ernst Röhm, the leader of the storm troopers and Hitler's longtime friend and right-hand man. Burger saw Adolf Hitler a number of times and even shook hands with him.

But about a year after Hitler came into power, on June 30, 1934, he decided to murder the storm troopers' leadership, including his friend Röhm. The storm troopers were too powerful, with a force of nearly three million men. And Hitler doubted that their leaders were loyal. He wanted absolute control and ordered his own personal bodyguard unit, the SS, to arrest and execute them without a trial. At the same time, the SS was ordered to kill several other political opponents and anyone whom Hitler believed had betrayed the Nazi movement. More than 1,000 people were arrested and an estimated two hundred were executed. It was only by chance that Burger wasn't murdered in what was later known as the "Night of the Long Knives."

Burger had been loaned as an aide-de-camp to the head of the medical division of the storm troopers, a former Olympian athlete and doctor named Emil Ketterer. Dr. Ketterer was a loyal Nazi who encouraged euthanizing people who were physically disabled. He was one of the few who escaped the massacre because Hitler still trusted him. And since Burger was with him, he was spared from certain death.

But nobody trusted the storm troopers after the massacre, and people would spit on their uniforms while passing them on the street. One man riding a bicycle called Burger a traitor, and Burger responded by shooting him off his bike.

After cheating death, Burger was assigned to Germany's political division, where he worked on journalism and propaganda for the Nazis. But a few years later, in 1939, after the Nazis invaded Poland, trouble caught up with him.

"I went to Poland as a special reporter to observe general conditions in Poland, and also to observe the war activities of [Nazi] party officials," Burger said.

Burger prepared a confidential report, criticizing the Nazi officials in Poland. He also sent a telegram, which someone read. Soon after, the Gestapo arrested Burger on trumped-up charges. One of the charges was the falsification of documents.

Burger was interrogated and locked up in a cell where prisoners were held when they were about to be executed.

Even though the Department of Justice eventually dropped the charges, the Gestapo still held him. Burger was confined to a crowded cell with sixty other prisoners. There were no windows, and they were allowed out to exercise for only ten minutes every two weeks. He was there for a year.

Before his release from prison, he had to sign a confidentiality document. Burger was not allowed to speak of his experience with the Gestapo. Then he was ordered to report to the German Army to be enlisted as a private with no chance for a promotion. But before he reported to his new job as a prison guard, he went to the Abwehr headquarters, and offered his services in any capacity in the United States. He wanted to get out of Germany and away from the Gestapo. Burger had lived in Milwaukee, Wisconsin, for many years working as a machinist. During that time, he had also become an American citizen.

Not long after, Walter Kappe sent him a letter. Kappe offered him the chance to "rehabilitate" his standing in the Nazi Party. This meant that Burger's record with the Gestapo would not be a mark against him or any of his family members. His personal honor would be restored.

Burger didn't hesitate. He seized the opportunity.

He was the last student to report to Quenz Farm. Dasch showed him around the estate and noted that he had the look of a haunted man. The burn marks on Burger's hands and legs were hard to miss.

Burger decided to be forthright with Dasch about his trouble with the Gestapo. But Dasch already knew and told Burger they could talk about it later. However, when the other saboteurs heard the rumor that Burger had spent time in a concentration camp, no one trusted him.

Eventually, Kappe sensed the tension and made an announcement to the class. He confirmed that Burger had been in the hands of the Gestapo. But Kappe stressed that he had complete confidence in Burger. He trusted Burger; therefore, everyone else should. But instead of creating trust, Kappe's statement simply raised more questions.

Burger, who was better versed in the political intricacies of the Nazi regime than the others, explained the infighting among the organizations for power and dominance. The saboteurs were working for the German government, not the Gestapo, which was a separate entity. Furthermore, the saboteurs were part of the Abwehr, which was also separate from the Gestapo. In fact, the Abwehr was in competition with the Gestapo. And there was so much animosity between the Abwehr and the Gestapo that they weren't allowed to frequent many of the same places because it would result in fights.

Even though Burger made it clear that as a saboteur he was actually working against the Gestapo, some of the saboteurs still didn't trust him. Herbert Haupt was one of them. Burger had told Haupt about the horrors he had seen and suffered at the hands of the Gestapo, expressing his bitter hatred. This made Haupt suspicious of Burger's motivations for returning to the United States and raised doubts about his loyalty to the Fatherland and the men on the sabotage mission.

The feelings of distrust were mutual. Burger didn't think much of Haupt. Despite Haupt's gregarious, life-of-the-party attitude, Burger saw something sinister in him. Haupt was powerfully built and an accomplished fighter in both wrestling and boxing. Like Dasch, Burger noticed that Haupt was "cunning." But he didn't think Haupt was intelligent, and felt he was overly interested in money. Burger believed this combination made Haupt "very dangerous."

The instructors at Hitler's school for sabotage agreed and warned the other saboteurs to keep a sharp eye on Haupt. They believed that Haupt's extreme interest in money made him vulnerable to bribes. And they suspected that if the opportunity to double-cross the mission presented itself, Haupt would seize the chance.

The leader of the second team, Edward Kerling, was also worried about Haupt. He would be in charge of Haupt when they landed off the Florida coast near Jacksonville. Kerling, who, like Haupt, was a "snappy" dresser, proudly wore a gold pin on his uniform. The gold pin indicated that he was a long-standing Nazi. He voiced his concerns to Kappe, complaining that Haupt wasn't serious enough.

That wasn't all. Kerling was also worried about another member on his team, his friend Hermann Neubauer. Kerling and Neubauer had met when they lived in America. Kerling had worked as a chauffeur, and Neubauer had worked mainly as a cook. When the war broke out in Germany, the two pooled their money with some other German friends and bought a boat. They tried to sail to Germany, but the Coast Guard intercepted.

The German government eventually helped them return to Germany in 1940. Upon their return, Kerling joined the army. He was assigned to a listening post, and later he worked for the Ministry of Propaganda.

But Neubauer was drafted into the army and sent to battle against Russia. Only three days in as a soldier, an artillery shell exploded near him. Shrapnel was embedded over his right eye, and the doctors couldn't remove it because the fragments were too close to his brain. Another piece, the size of a dime, was lodged in his cheek.

Neubauer had been in the hospital when he received a letter from Kappe asking him if he wanted to go on an assignment to America. Neubauer accepted. But Kerling thought his friend wasn't right in the head after fighting on the front lines. He described Neubauer as having "splinters on top of his brain" from his war wound.

Kappe disregarded Kerling's complaints. Neubauer was a soldier willing to follow orders. And Kappe believed that Haupt's physical strength, his background in boxing, and his American ways would serve the mission well.

As the days and weeks passed, the saboteurs got to know one another a little better. But instead of bonding into a tightly united team, no one seemed to like or trust the other.

Burger thought Dasch talked too much, and he noticed Dasch didn't get along with anyone. When it was necessary to stand at attention and "Heil Hitler," Dasch kept his hands in his pockets. Burger suspected that Dasch was trying to see how far he could push back against the school's authorities without getting fired.

Burger wasn't the only one who noticed. Some of the others were suspicious too. Quirin, who looked like Dasch's brother, didn't like or trust Dasch at all. He feared Dasch wasn't fit for the mission and the best way to deal with him was to kill him. Others, like Kerling, Kappe, and the instructors were just concerned that Dasch wasn't paying attention.

During the lectures and labs, the men were allowed to take notes, but at the end of the course, the notes were going to be collected and destroyed. So the men had to memorize formulas and procedures. But Dasch was nervous and, as the leader, he felt a lot of pressure. He didn't have a strong science background and didn't know much about chemicals. He was having trouble learning the subject because he didn't have much interest in it. If he liked something, he learned it. But if he didn't like it, he didn't make much effort.

He told Kappe that "It would be enough if the others learned their lessons perfectly." Dasch figured since he was the leader, he could order the others on his team to do what was needed. "I am the boss when I get there," Dasch told Kappe.

Kerling didn't like Dasch's lackadaisical attitude toward their studies, and he hounded Dasch about learning the formulas.

"I made the mistake of taking the whole thing too lightly," Dasch later said. "During those three weeks at Quenz I acted just like a jackass."

But Dasch could get away with it because Kappe had confidence in Dasch's knowledge and expertise of America, which was an invaluable asset to the mission. The other saboteurs noticed that Dasch was Kappe's favorite, and resented that "Kappe did whatever Dasch wanted, and Dasch could do anything he wanted at school."

On the last day of school, the men were tested. The saboteurs were given instructions about where their target was and, at night, they were to assess its most vulnerable spot. Then they were to go to the laboratory, make their bomb, and blow up the target. Their instructors watched while the men tried to be stealthy and set off their bombs. "Guards" stood by with firecrackers and were ready to throw them at the saboteurs if they were seen. "Mines" were placed to set off firecrackers or trigger tear gas. Burger was the only one who wasn't seen by the guards, and he didn't step on any firecrackers or set off tear gas. But Kappe was very satisfied with the teams. Everyone had remained calm and cool through the entire exercise.

To finalize their training, the saboteurs took field trips to become more familiar with the type of targets in their planned sabotage. In Berlin they toured the canal system and learned the best way to destroy a lock, which was integral to the raising and lowering of the water levels while transporting supplies.

Reinhold Barth, Dasch's relative and Kappe's right-hand man, had worked for the Long Island Rail Road in America, and he gave them a tour of a railroad plant and yards. He showed them where they should plant the bombs to blow up railroads, such as tunnels, bridges, switches, and brakes. He even gave them instructions on how to operate a train engine, just in case. And Barth explained how the exploding "coal" could be mixed in with the real coal, which would unwittingly be tossed into the furnace.

They toured I.G. Farben, the aluminum and magnesium plant in Frankfurt. As they inspected the factory and learned the best way to cut the power supply, Dasch noticed that the "foreign labor" at the plant was actually the Nazi version of "slave labor."

"I found that the majority of the workers employed at all plants were either prisoners of war or German military prisoners or Russians," Dasch said. When he was at the railroad plant and yards, he asked the foreman, "How are these poor people keeping alive? They appear to me to be starved."

"To hell with them," the foreman said. "They drop down just like flies."

Dasch noticed young people, no more than fifteen or sixteen years old, wearing heavy fur pieces even though it wasn't cold outside. He asked the foreman why they were bundled up.

"They wear everything they possess," the foreman replied. "They go to bed with it and they go to work with it."

Dasch felt sickened. He still secretly supported labor unions and workers' rights. He "couldn't understand how men could be so inhuman." But he'd lived in Nazi Germany long enough to be wary of protesting openly about his beliefs that conflicted with the Nazi regime's agenda.

A few months ago, when Dasch was in Kappe's office in Berlin, a German intelligence officer talked about the mass execution of 35,000 Jews in Kiev, Ukraine. He explained how the Jews were rounded up into groups of two to three hundred people and ordered to dig a huge hole in the ground. Afterward, they were shot with a bullet to the back of their heads so they would fall into the hole that was their grave. The German intelligence officer laughed when he said,

"The trigger finger of the executing officers became tired."

While Dasch listened to the story, his "stomach turned." At that moment, he didn't know what to do, but he thought they were "the dirtiest bastards on earth." He turned to Kappe and said, "For Christ sake, this is an awful war and this is an awful way to kill people."

Kappe called Dasch "chicken-hearted," and said, "What kind of German are you? We Germans have one mission, which is to kill all the Jews."

Dasch learned never to object to such matters again.

After they finished touring the plant, their sabotage training was almost complete. As a precaution, each saboteur had to sign a contract and pledge that he would do his best for the Fatherland. They were sworn to secrecy. Disclosing information about their secret mission was punishable by death. And any person they told about the mission could face the death penalty as well.

To completely ensure the men didn't double-cross the Nazi regime, they were warned that Gestapo agents had infiltrated the FBI. Therefore, if any one of them went to the FBI, the Gestapo would know and target them and their families. They were told that there were agents from Hitler's Secret Service whose sole job was to secretly watch them to make sure they were doing their job.

Before the saboteurs were to go off on their mission, Colonel Erwin von Lahousen, the chief of intelligence, hosted a dinner in the elegant private dining room of the Zoo Restaurant. Lahousen gave a speech, telling the saboteurs that if they were successful, they could do more damage than the soldiers on the front lines. Their sabotage work could decide the outcome of the war.

It was after midnight when the dinner and speeches were finished. The men lingered, talking to one another in small groups. Lahousen took Dasch aside. He warned Dasch to trust no one, and told Dasch that it was his secret duty to kill any traitor in the group.

Dasch understood. He was the boss.

On May 26, 1942, at 6:00 p.m., George Dasch and his team boarded a freighter, crossed its deck, and walked carefully over a gangplank into German U-boat 202. Kerling and his team had left earlier on a U-boat headed to Florida. It would take them nearly three weeks to arrive on the eastern shores of America.

Kappe had wished them good luck. Operation

Pastorius had been carefully planned. Kappe had cleverly chosen to name this mission after Daniel Pastorius, a German educator. Pastorius had emigrated to America in 1683 and founded Germantown, Pennsylvania.

Kappe had plans to create his own "Germantown," only bigger. A third team of saboteurs was to follow soon after the first two teams were established. Then more teams after that. And Kappe himself planned on returning to America to oversee his budding Nazi nation. As the person in charge of the school for sabotage, Kappe had made sure that the men were well trained. Failure was not an option.

"The sabotage expedition was better equipped with sabotage apparatus and better trained than any other expedition . . . The German Secret Service attached the greatest importance to the success of the Undertaking," Lord Rothschild, a British secret agent with MI5, would later report.

But there was one fatal flaw Kappe had overlooked. The saboteurs didn't trust one another. And they were right not to, because one of them was going to betray the others. And it was going to cost them their lives.

THE NAZI SABOTEURS

Team 1
LONG ISLAND, NEW YORK LANDING

LEADER

NAME

George John Dasch

ALIAS

George Davis

CODE NAME

Stritch (means "dash" in German)

DESCRIPTION

Thin with a long face and sporty appearance. Dark hair with a noticeable streak of gray. Lived in America for nearly twenty years. Was in the German Army and, briefly, the U.S. Army. Mainly worked as a waiter. Not a member of the Nazi Party. Not an American citizen. Speaks English well with a penchant for slang. Usually wears a hat and keeps one hand in his pocket or holds a newspaper. Married to an American. Wife interned in Bermuda.

NAME
(Ernest) Peter Burger

ALIAS
No alias.

DESCRIPTION
Dark brown hair. Noticeable burn mark scars on his hands and legs. Dresses nicely. Speaks English slowly and clearly with an accent. Born in Germany but lived in America and became a U.S. citizen. Worked as a machinist. Long-standing member of the Nazi Party. Was a storm trooper. Avoided getting killed in a massacre but arrested by Gestapo on falsified charges. Spent nearly two years in a prison camp. Released and offered the chance to "rehabilitate" his standing in the Nazi Party. Wife lives in Germany.

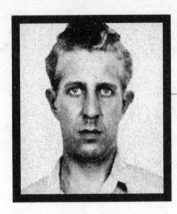

NAME

Richard Quirin

ALIAS

Richard Quintas

DESCRIPTION

Gray hair that is turning white. Slender build. Slouches. Looks similar to George Dasch, and many ask if they are brothers. They are not. He dislikes Dasch and wants to kill him. Quirin is intelligent, audacious, and loyal to the Nazi Party. Speaks English with a slight accent. In America, Quirin worked as a handyman, chauffeur, and mechanic. In Germany, he worked as a tool and die maker at Volkswagen with fellow saboteur Heinrich Heinck. Quirin is married, and his wife and child live in Germany.

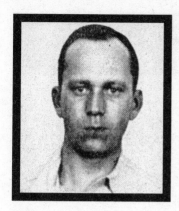

NAME

Heinrich Heinck

ALIAS

Henry Kaynor

DESCRIPTION

Heavy build; very thin, light blond hair. There's a mark in the middle of his forehead from a piece of iron that flew from a machine in a factory. Speaks in a low voice with a German accent. Seems unsure of himself and has difficulty making decisions. First met Walter Kappe when they lived in America. Friends with Richard Quirin. Worked in various American factories before returning to Germany and working at Volkswagen. Heinck thinks Dasch is intelligent. Dasch thinks Heinck is a dumb and big-mouthed coward.

Team 2
PONTE VEDRA, FLORIDA LANDING

LEADER

NAME

Edward Kerling

ALIAS

Edward Kelly

DESCRIPTION

His dark blond hair is often styled in an American haircut, parted on the left side and swept back. He speaks fast with near-perfect English, although Dasch can hear an accent if he listens closely. Always smiling. The FBI describes him as a "dirty rat" and a "snappy dresser." Loves two women who live in America. Wears a special gold pin that signals he is a loyal and long-standing Nazi. Worked as a butler and chauffeur before returning to Germany. His German wife lives in America.

NAME

Herbert Hans Haupt

ALIAS

Larry Jordan

CODE NAME

Bingo

DESCRIPTION

Good-looking with dark wavy hair, which he combs back and coats with brilliantine. Snazzy dresser. Speaks perfect English. Was born in Germany but grew up in America and is an American citizen. Worked as an optician's apprentice. Ran off to Mexico to avoid his pregnant girlfriend and ended up in Germany. Earned two German medals for running a British blockade. Girl crazy. Can be found carelessly spending money in restaurants and nightclubs. Always looking for a good time. But some think that hiding underneath his fun-loving personality is a very dangerous and cunning man.

NAME

Werner Thiel

ALIAS

William Thomas

DESCRIPTION

Stout, but recently lost weight. Half bald but remaining hair is dark brown and slicked back. High forehead, square jaw, and dimple on chin. Speaks in a slow monotone and avoids looking at the person. Shabby dresser. Met Kappe in America and met Dasch on the voyage from U.S. to Germany. Thiel doesn't like or trust Dasch. Worked in two large automobile factories (General Motors and Ford) in Detroit as a tool and die maker. Upon returning to Germany, he was drafted into the army.

NAME

Hermann Otto Neubauer

ALIAS

Herman Nicholas

CODE NAME

Koch (German for "cook")

DESCRIPTION

"A typical gangster type." Strong and husky build. Has dark brown hair and used to have a mustache before shaving it off. There's a noticeable scar on the side of his face near his temple. Always wears a hat pulled down over his eyes. Speaks English with a strong accent. Main occupation was a cook. Recently he was a soldier and was sent to the Russian front, where he was wounded by shrapnel. He's a good friend of Kerling's who described him as having "splinters on top of his brain" from his war wound. Was a member of the German American Bund. He is married to an American, and she lives unhappily in Germany with her in-laws.

THE SABOTAGE TARGETS

The **ALUMINUM CORPORATION OF AMERICA** (Alcoa) plants in Alcoa, Tennessee; Massena, New York; and East St. Louis, Illinois.

Pennsylvania Salt Manufacturing Company's **CRYOLITE PLANT** in Philadelphia.

The main line of the **CHESAPEAKE AND OHIO RAILROAD** at any vulnerable point.

The **CANAL SYSTEM** on the Ohio River near Cincinnati to Louisville, Kentucky.

THE HELL GATE BRIDGE on the Pennsylvania Railroad that connected Astoria, Queens, to Randall's Island, Manhattan.

The **NEW YORK CITY WATER SUPPLY.**

HYDROELECTRIC PLANTS in Niagara Falls.

Railroad tracks on **"HORSESHOE CURVE"** near Altoona, Pennsylvania.

The **PENNSYLVANIA RAILROAD DEPOT** in Newark, New Jersey.

LUGGAGE LOCKERS in railroad depots.

JEWISH-OWNED DEPARTMENT STORES, such as Macy's.

PART TWO

TWO

The Mission

Chapter 4

BEACHED

June 13, 1942
Amagansett, Long Island, New York

It was after midnight when the gray U-boat surfaced off the coast of Amagansett, Long Island. It was too dark and foggy to see the porcupine painted on the side of the submarine's tower. A rubber dinghy was lowered onto the choppy waves. Four waterproof wooden boxes were loaded onto the bobbing boat. Inside each wooden box was another tin box. Three of the tin boxes were carefully packed with explosives. The fourth box contained dynamite, which was disguised to look like lumps of coal, incendiary pencils, timing devices, fuses, primers, wire, screws, and sulfuric acid.

George Dasch and his team stepped off the U-boat and squeezed onto the dinghy. They had brought along a couple of short-handled trench shovels, a duffel bag packed with American clothes, and a suitcase with money sewn in its lining. Burger carried the suitcase, but it belonged to Dasch, who was in charge of handling the money.

The mission was well funded with a total of $172,200 divided between the two teams. (In today's dollars, the amount is worth over $2.5 million.) Dasch had carefully distributed a large amount of money to his team the day before the landing. Each person was given $4,000, which they hid in their money belts. Everyone also received about four hundred dollars in small bills for pocket change.

Despite the large sum they carried, there were still money problems. No one was completely sure if their money could be traced back to the German government. And dollar bills that were backed by the gold standard, which were no longer in circulation, had been found mixed in. When they discovered these errors, the saboteurs were angry that Kappe didn't seem worried about how easily the bills could be traced back to them. The morale of both groups was so low that the mission was almost called off.

But it was all the money Kappe could get his hands on, so after heated discussions, everyone finally relented. They weeded out the gold certificates and decided to avoid handing a clerk more than one fifty-dollar bill at a time.

Along with the money, Kappe was able to obtain uniforms for his saboteurs, the same ones that the crew members on the submarine wore. They'd been issued a pair of khaki pants, a khaki jacket minus the shiny buttons, black leather shoes, gray wool socks, a black belt, and a hat with a swastika on the front. In Kappe's final instructions, he told the saboteurs to wear the uniform on the U-boat and when landing. He explained that if they wore civilian clothes and were captured, they risked being executed as spies. If they were caught while in uniform, they would be treated as prisoners of war.

But they didn't plan on getting caught. Two German sailors, who were armed with light submachine guns and carbines, were with them. Orders were given that if the team ran into anyone on the beach, they were to overpower them. Before the men prepared to head to shore, the captain of the U-boat said, "You bring the bodies back and we'll feed them to the fish when we get out to sea again."

The rough waves and dense fog made it nearly impossible to navigate the dinghy. They weren't entirely sure if they were landing in their planned spot of East Hampton. At this point, no one was even certain if they were heading toward the beach or back out to sea. Luckily, the dinghy was attached to the submarine with a tow line, and they had a flare gun. The sailors had a lifeline to the U-boat.

Even so, big waves rolled in, and the small rubber boat was tossed around and around in a circle. Cold salt water rushed in, filling the boat and soaking the men. But they all paddled furiously, hoping their feet would soon touch land.

For the past seventeen days, everyone on the team— except for slow-witted Heinck—had suffered from seasickness. They had learned the hard way that the U-boat, which was about the size of a school bus inside, traveled mostly above water across the Atlantic. While surfaced, the U-boat could travel faster—at about the speed of a bicycle. But it was a bumpy and nauseating ride—not to mention crowded.

There were forty men on the crew and six officers. Except for the captain, no one knew they were trans- porting saboteurs on a secret mission to America. They were told that Dasch and his team were war correspon- dents. The crew was instructed not to speak to them.

Although Dasch and his men were allowed to move freely through the U-boat, it was difficult to walk around much because it was too jam-packed.

The U-boat carried fourteen torpedoes. In the bow of the submarine, there were four torpedoes, and in the stern there was one torpedo tube for the remaining ten torpedoes. It was also armed with a cannon, and behind the tower there was an antiaircraft gun, loaded with a magazine of ten shells. The bullets were tracers. The crew was armed with rifles and pistols.

The U-boat was divided into three sections. The diesel and electric motors were in the stern. In the center of the sub, there was the control room, and the tower was directly above it. The tower was accessed from an iron ladder in the control room. In the first part of the tower, there was the steering room where the periscope was operated. Directly above, there was the hatch, and when it was opened there was access to a platform on the tower of the U-boat.

Dasch and Burger were assigned to the officers' quarters in the forward part of the submarine. But Quirin and Heinck were assigned to the crew's quarters, where they had to wait until a bed was available before they could lie down to sleep.

Dasch's team wasn't just physically divided. Quirin disliked and distrusted Dasch so much that he still wanted to kill him. It became obvious to many on the small sub that Quirin and Heinck had formed an alliance that excluded Dasch and Burger. Heinck had grown dependent on Quirin, his friend and former coworker at Volkswagen. And as the U-boat inched closer to their landing spot, the rift continued to widen.

"Richard Quirin and Heinrich Heinck seemed to get very well acquainted and make plans of their own," Burger said. "Whenever George [Dasch] and I approached them while they were talking, they would shut up. This was noticeable even to the officers of the submarine."

The crammed quarters magnified the tension, fear, and distrust. It was so bad that Heinck was worried he was going to have a nervous breakdown. And Quirin was afraid Heinck might talk if he was arrested or drank too much. It was a well-founded concern. Prior to leaving, Heinck had gone to a bar, gotten blitzed, and announced he was a German secret agent. Since then, Quirin was keeping a close watch on his friend, trying to look out for him.

Heinck's growing fear and apprehension was

obvious to others. They were worried that he would cause problems for them. Burger described him as being in a relentless "state of fear throughout our entire trip to the United States." And Dasch thought Heinck was a loudmouthed coward.

Regardless, there was no turning back now. So Dasch made an effort to boost his men's morale. The captain had informed him that the image of the porcupine on the side of the sub's tower was technically against regulations. But they were allowed to keep it because the porcupine boosted everyone's spirits, uniting them. The captain and crew also wore a porcupine emblem on their hats for good luck. This gave Dasch an idea.

He wanted to unite his own team and have them view him as their esteemed leader, like the U-boat crew viewed their captain. So Dasch asked a crewman to cut some thin tin into the image of the porcupine. Dasch then gave each saboteur a tiny porcupine in honor of their voyage across the Atlantic Ocean. The tin porcupine was to be used as a sign, a way of communicating without speaking, when they secretly met, indicating that everything and everyone was all right.

Dasch's grand gesture was a bust. The porcupine pin didn't unite or change anyone's opinion about one another. Still, good luck seemed to be on their side as they huddled together in the dinghy. Despite the fog and violent waves rocking their rubber boat, they somehow managed to row their way to the shore. The two sailors hopped out and dragged the boat up onto the beach. The saboteurs quickly began

John Cullen.

unloading the waterproof boxes. Dasch stepped out and walked in a wide circle, trying to look through the fog. From what he could see, which wasn't much, the coast was clear. He had no idea that John Cullen, the coast guardsman, was walking toward him in the fog.

In the meantime, Heinck, Quirin, and Burger carried the wooden boxes, the bag of clothes, and the suitcase full of money up a sand dune. Grabbing the shovels, they quickly threw some sand over the boxes, trying to camouflage them until they could dig a hole and bury them. But first, they hastily changed out of their grayish-brown military uniforms and into their

American clothes. Kappe had told them to bring a complete suit that was made in America to change into and wear, so they would blend in.

Some of the men didn't have enough American-made clothes. Although clothes were hard to obtain in Germany, Kappe offered to use his access to a two-story warehouse that was well stocked with suits, overcoats, raincoats, hats, underwear, luggage, shoes, and boots. There was every size from a variety of countries—America, Czechoslovakia, Poland, France, and others. But the clothes in the warehouse weren't new. They had been seized from thousands of captured, imprisoned, and dead men.

But rather than take Kappe's offer, the men had each taken inventory of their wardrobe and made exchanges, finding enough suitable clothing among themselves. Dasch had brought three pairs of American shoes to Germany, so he gave one pair away. He also gave away an extra pair of pants. Kerling gave another member an entire suit.

Burger, who, like the others, was wearing a bathing suit, shoved his uniform into the canvas bag along with Quirin's and Heinck's discarded navy fatigues. He took the bag and dragged it down the sand dune through the fog. Part of the plan was to give the bag to the sailors, so they could take it back on board the U-boat. As Burger approached the water, he could hear Dasch's voice over the crash of the waves. As he walked closer, he saw that Dasch was speaking to one of the sailors. Or so he thought.

Burger went up behind the sailor and said to Dasch, "You're certainly a fast worker." But Burger didn't say it in English. He said it in German.

"Shut up!" Dasch yelled as he grabbed Burger's mouth, covering it with his hand.

Burger suddenly realized his mistake. Dasch wasn't speaking to one of the German sailors. Dasch was talking to an American coast guardsman.

"Don't you see, everything is all right." Dasch spoke to Burger in English. "Go back with the boys and stay with them."

Dasch gripped coast guardsman John Cullen's arm, and they walked a few feet away. He could tell Cullen was scared. And for good reason. Dasch had just threatened Cullen's life, telling him, "Well, I wouldn't want to have to kill you."

Dasch took a moment to consider this "very ticklish

problem." If Dasch were to follow the captain of the U-boat's orders and overpower the coast guardsman, he would have to lure him to the dinghy. That way, the two sailors could help and then take the man back to the submarine. But Dasch didn't like that idea. He didn't want to kill anyone. Even so, he didn't want to go back to the Coast Guard station. It would be tough to explain what they were doing on the beach, especially with the bags and boxes of explosives.

Dasch was visibly nervous, and he was worried the other men were "losing their heads." So, despite his orders to kill, he decided to use "a little psychology."

"Forget about this," Dasch said, reaching into his pocket. "And I will give you some money and you can have a good time."

"I don't want any money," Cullen said, refusing the bribe.

"Take this," Dasch said, offering three hundred dollars.

After witnessing Dasch's angry outburst, Cullen was wondering how many more men were hidden in the fog. He was armed with only a flashlight and flare gun. So, Cullen reached out and took the money, worried they would kill him if he didn't.

"Good!" Dasch said, then told him to count it.

"No," Cullen said. "That's all right." It was too dark to see it anyway, so he put it in his pocket.

"Now wait a minute," Dasch said, taking off his brown fedora hat. "Take a good look at me."

Cullen tried to take a good look. He turned on his flashlight, the beam shining into Dasch's narrow face. He noticed a streak of gray hair.

"Look into my eyes," Dasch demanded. "Look into my eyes." Then he put his hat back on and said, "I'll be meeting you in East Hampton sometime. Do you know me?"

"No, sir. I never saw you before in my life."

"My name is George Davis," Dasch said. "What's your name?"

"Frank Collins," he lied.

Cullen began to back up, keeping his eyes on Dasch. As soon as Dasch turned his back, Cullen ran for his life, disappearing into the fog.

With the coast guardsman gone, Dasch waded back to the sailors, who had been busy looking for their lost paddles and emptying the water from the dinghy. He told them to head back to the U-boat, forgetting to hand over the bag of German uniforms. Dasch then made his way through the fog toward his team. It was about one o'clock, and the fog was thinning a bit. He couldn't help but feel a sense of satisfaction with his quick thinking. Dasch felt a surge of pride that he was able "to fool that little Navy boy."

When he reached the men on his team, they were shaken and upset. And very suspicious of Dasch for not following orders to kill the coast guardsman. Despite this, Dasch confidently assured them that he had "buffaloed" the man.

But then a red flare shot up into the misty sky. The men ducked and fell to the ground, taking cover. Searchlights glowed in the fog, trying to scan the area.

"They're looking for us and it's all your fault, George. You should have killed that guy on the beach or we should have done it! I ought to kill you right now. If I had a gun, I would," Quirin said.

Despite his fraying nerves, Dasch remembered the captain of the U-boat telling him the sailors had a flare in case they had trouble getting back to the submarine.

"Now, boys, this is the time to be quiet and hold your nerves. Do exactly what I tell you," Dasch said, taking charge. "Each of you get a box and follow me."

The men followed, and Dasch led them over a couple of sand dunes before coming upon a gulch. He stopped and told them to put down the cargo and dig a hole. When the hole was big, they placed the four boxes into it. They carefully covered the boxes with sand and seaweed. Another hole was dug in a different spot and the bag of uniforms was buried.

The plan was to come back for the explosives several weeks later. First, they'd been instructed to buy a farm or a business, which was to be used as a "front" to cover up their illegal activities and as a place to hide the explosives.

Dasch needed to change out of his wet military pants before leading the team to the train depot. He was told that they had accidentally left his clothes behind near their landing spot. Dasch was furious, calling them a "bunch of bums." He noticed Burger and Heinck were "shivering like a bunch of kids."

"Lay down and keep quiet," Dasch ordered. He and Quirin started retracing where they'd been along the top of the sand dunes and finally found Dasch's clothes.

They returned, and after Dasch changed into a pair of gray checkered golf pants, the men crouched down and waited.

It was a while before they were comfortable that the coast was clear. Finally, the saboteurs began moving, crawling, then walking away from the crashing waves.

At the time, Dasch didn't realize that he'd lost his notebook on the beach. It was filled with names and addresses of people who could identify him. In fact, in the mad rush, numerous items had been dropped or haphazardly buried by the saboteurs. A pack of German cigarettes. A bottle of German schnapps. A German Army cap with a swastika. A brown gabardine vest. An overcoat. A shovel. A torn identification card.

And someone had left a trail in the sand leading to the buried boxes.

Five minutes after John Cullen ran into George Dasch on the beach, he burst through the door of the Coast Guard station.

"There are Germans on the beach!" he shouted. "Let's go!"

His comrades were startled awake. At first no one

believed him. Until he showed them the money Dasch had given him.

Each man grabbed a rifle, but only one knew how to use them. After a quick lesson, they ran out onto the beach and started combing it for Nazis. Fifteen minutes later, there was a small parting in the fog, and the silhouette of a U-boat appeared about 150 feet from shore. There was a roar and a steady chugging noise. The smell of burning diesel fuel wafted through the salty air. Fearing another landing of more Nazis, the coast guardsmen moved behind the sand dunes with orders to resist an invasion.

But soon, it was quiet, with just the sound of the crashing waves rolling in and rolling out. The U-boat was gone, and the Nazis had escaped. The coast guardsmen searched the beach, but the saboteurs were gone too. They weren't far away, hiding in some scrub grass near a road, trying to remain calm, but Heinck kept whispering, "We're surrounded."

When daylight finally came, the saboteurs continued on their way to the train station. In the meantime, the Coast Guard discovered the items the men had dropped on the beach. And, most important, they found the trail in the sand leading to the buried boxes.

Within two hours of the U-boat landing, the Coast Guard alerted the FBI. But the FBI didn't take the report seriously. They received so many false reports of U-boat sightings that they dismissed this one as "dubious." Until hours later, that is, when they learned that the Coast Guard had uncovered boxes of explosives and German uniforms along the beach.

At 6:45 a.m., Ira Baker, the train station agent, opened the ticket window at the Amagansett train station. A man wearing a brown fedora hat and carrying a suitcase approached the window. He asked for four tickets to Jamaica in Queens, New York.

"The fishing hasn't been very good out here," the man said. "In fact, it's been miserable because of the fog, and I guess we'll go home."

Baker handed the man the tickets. He didn't notice that the man's gray golf pants were wet from the green bathing suit he'd worn underneath. And he couldn't see the man's mismatched knee socks.

Still, Baker did see him walk over to a group of three other men. The men were talking rapidly, but Baker couldn't hear what they were saying. The four men proceeded to the other side of the station to wait for the train. The man in the fedora hat purchased four newspapers, which he handed to the others.

At 6:57 a.m., the train rumbled out of the station. Once inside, the four Nazi saboteurs felt some relief. The initial danger of landing on the enemy's shore and being captured or shot was behind them. Still, they opened their newspapers and hid behind them. The front-page headline blared, "JAPANESE MAKE LANDINGS IN ALEUTIAN ISLANDS."

Later that day, Ira was cleaning up the station yard when he found a green bathing suit, a pair of white sneakers, a pair of white socks, and a shirt in the hedges. He gathered up the discarded clothes and put them in a box near the incinerator, so they could be burned.

Chapter 5

IN PLAIN SIGHT

Saturday, June 13, 1942
New York City

It was a scorching hot day in New York City. Along a three-and-a-half-mile stretch of Fifth Avenue, the flag-bedecked buildings with flat roofs, balconies, and fire escapes were stuffed with sweating spectators. Despite the lack of elbow room, they were busy tossing torn bits of paper over the side, creating a steady rain of confetti onto the "greatest and most significant" parade in New York City's history.

Below, on the overcrowded sidewalks, more than two and a half million people, armed with beach chairs, picnic baskets, and thermoses, solemnly watched hundreds of floats pass by. The all-day parade, titled Hitler Unlooses War, was a demonstration of America's military and industrial power, aiming to stamp out any doubt about America's ability to crush Hitler and win the war. Through a dramatic display of pageantry, it told how Hitler unleashed "the dogs of war upon the world." One of the many war-themed floats to pass by was called Hitler, the Axis War Monster. Men, women, and children watched as a mechanical dragon-like creature with a swastika painted on its armor trampled humans to death while a trumpet blared and a loud-speaker screeched, "Heil Hitler!"

The floats were followed by a procession of tanks, soldiers, sailors, marines, industrial workers, and others who were protecting America's home front. Overhead, American bombers and fighter planes thundered through the clear blue sky.

"It was a grand spectacle," Mayor Fiorello La Guardia said. "Its purpose was to show the world that New York is at war. It was necessary to show that by something more than words."

The organizers of the parade understood that such a spectacle might provoke an air raid or attack on New York City, so extra precautions were taken. Interceptor planes were kept on alert, and 10,000 policemen were assigned to guard against any acts of violence or sabotage by enemy agents.

But the enemy agents weren't at the parade. Hitler's Nazi saboteurs were a half mile away from the grandstand in Herald Square, eating at the Horn & Hardart

Horn & Hardart Automat, a secret meeting place for the Nazi saboteurs

Automat. The shiny chrome-and-glass cafeteria, where customers inserted nickels into a slot and turned a knob to open a glass door for their food, was one of George Dasch's favorite restaurants.

It was nearing three o'clock, and Dasch and Burger were waiting to meet up with Quirin and Heinck. They were sitting at a glossy table surrounded by shoe-box-sized compartments filled with freshly made cakes, pies, pastries, bread, sandwiches, fruit, salad, hot platters of macaroni and cheese, beef pies, and chicken pies, just a few of the automat's four hundred menu items.

The smell of Horn & Hardart's famous fresh-dripped coffee wafted through the air. It was an abundant contrast to the meager food rations in Nazi Germany. Dasch greedily ate two salads and a hearty slice of coconut cream pie. He washed it all down with a cold glass of milk. Dasch looked like all the other customers, blending right in. So did Burger.

They were each decked out in brand-new American clothes. When their train from Long Island had arrived at a stop in Queens, the men went shopping. They purchased some new pants, shirts, underwear, socks, and shoes, leaving their dirty and sandy clothes behind in their dressing rooms. For a nickel, they had their new

In Plain Sight

leather shoes shined and gave their old ones away to the shoe shiner.

When they finally arrived at Penn Station in Manhattan, overflowing with passengers heading to the war parade, Burger and Dasch, who had traveled the rest of the way separately, checked in to the nearby Hotel Governor Clinton. It was a luxury hotel in the heart of New York City's garment district, where a plethora of Jewish-owned department stores sold their wares. One of them was Macy's, the world's largest department store and sponsor of the Macy's Thanksgiving Day Parade.

Dasch and Burger went inside the Edwardian-styled building with an art deco tower and rode the wooden escalator to the men's department, located on the second floor. Already known for having quality merchandise with the best prices, Macy's "flexikool" leisure suit, made of washable spun rayon, was available in blue, tan, and rust colors for a "kool" $9.92 ($153.90 in today's dollars). Slip-on loafer shoes were a bargain at $4.94 ($76.51 in today's dollars), and genuine pigskin wallets in black and brown were $1.98 ($30.66 in today's dollars).

With more than $80,000 ($1.2 million in today's

dollars) in their possession, the men were having fun spending it freely on another shopping spree. Unlike the strict clothes rationing in Germany, the men cheerfully bought more shirts, pants, underwear, socks, and a suitcase. Dasch splurged on a new wristwatch, and even bought a new handkerchief for twenty-five cents despite already having one. The handkerchief he had brought with him from Germany wasn't to be used for a runny nose or wiping away tears.

Dasch's handkerchief held the names of the saboteurs' contacts in America, written in invisible ink. One name was Father Carl Krepper, a German-born Lutheran pastor and Nazi spy in New Jersey. He could help them with any fake identification papers. Another name was Walter Froehling, in Chicago. He was Herbie Haupt's uncle, and he could help them find a hideout for the boxes of explosives. The handkerchief also contained an address in Lisbon, Portugal, that they could use if they needed to contact Walter Kappe. If anyone was ever arrested, they were to write a letter to one of the contacts on the handkerchief and say, "My dear" and then the name of their contact. "My dear" was the secret signal to whoever the letter was addressed to that the writer had been caught. It was Dasch's idea to use the secret code, and he thought it was just one of his many great ideas.

As Dasch was finishing up his pie and milk at the automat, feeling satisfied that he no longer had to worry about going hungry anymore like he did in Germany, he saw two men wearing flashy striped jackets with their shirts unbuttoned at the collar walking toward them. One of them was slouching. And one of them was carrying a new suitcase. It was Heinck and Quirin. They too had gone shopping, momentarily forgetting their persistent fear, and had fun stocking up on new American clothes. Dasch wasn't convinced that they'd made good fashion choices. Nazi saboteurs were supposed to blend in, not stand out. So Dasch told them they looked "neat" in a sarcastic tone.

Not giving them time to respond to his jab, Dasch told them to get something to eat. When they returned to the table with food piled on their plates, Dasch said, "Aren't you glad to be back in the United States?" Everyone on the team was finally in agreement on something. There was a collective feeling of relief that they hadn't been captured during the landing. And they were enjoying their freedom.

Dasch reminded them that they were not to commit any sabotage until both teams were settled in America. Before beginning the mission, Dasch had argued furiously with Kappe that the saboteurs were to spend a few months acclimating and blending in before blowing up any of their targets. Kappe had argued that it wasn't necessary to wait but finally relented.

The next order of business Dasch wanted to discuss with them was their hotel. He suggested to Quirin and Heinck to check in to the nearby Hotel Chesterfield, just off Broadway on Forty-Ninth Street. They would meet again tomorrow, Sunday, at one o'clock at the Chalet Suisse restaurant. But if, for some reason, Dasch didn't show up, they would meet at Grant's Tomb at six o'clock.

After the meeting broke up, Quirin and Heinck didn't check into the Hotel Chesterfield. They chose a different one. Quirin and Heinck still didn't trust Dasch, especially after he failed to overpower the coast guardsman like he was instructed. So, using their aliases, Richard Quintas and Henry Kaynor, they registered at the Martinique, a deluxe hotel on Forty-Ninth Street. That way, Dasch couldn't find them, if they didn't want to be found.

While Dasch and his team were busy shopping and meeting at the Horn & Hardart Automat, the FBI was examining the boxes of explosives and equipment the Coast Guard had discovered on Amagansett Beach. Eugene Connelley, the assistant FBI director, declared it was the "most impressive" sabotage equipment he had ever seen. And Don Parsons, a top-notch explosives expert, determined the cache of explosives and equipment would have caused millions of dollars of destruction to America's war industry. FBI agents were sent to stake out the beach in case the saboteurs returned.

Later that day, George Dasch and Peter Burger were sitting at a table with fine china, silverware, and crisp white linen napkins. Overhead, crystal chandeliers sparkled like stars in the soft evening light. They were reading the dinner menu in one of the Hotel Governor Clinton's three restaurants, the Coral Room.

The menu was diverse, offering everything from fried frog legs with tartar sauce to sautéed split jumbo squab (also known as pigeon) to charcoal-broiled sirloin steak and filet mignon. Plus, there was a choice of buttered carrots, lima beans, french-fried onions, and potatoes au gratin.

It was an easy decision. They ordered thick juicy steaks for $2.50 apiece. It was a meal they couldn't have eaten in Nazi Germany with the strict food rationing and meat shortages.

The restaurant wasn't very crowded, especially for a Saturday night. So, during dinner they quietly discussed the various jobs they'd been ordered to do in America. Burger had been instructed to move to Chicago, the location chosen for their headquarters. Since Burger was an accomplished artist and violin player, he was instructed to set up a studio and advertise his services as a commercial artist in the *Chicago Tribune* newspaper. He was to include his address in the classified ad. That way, the other saboteurs had one more way to contact one another, as a last resort.

They also discussed the political situation in Germany. Dasch revealed to Burger some of the hardships his family was experiencing, and Burger disclosed more details about his difficulties with the Gestapo. When Burger finished, Dasch had more to say, which wasn't unusual for the loquacious leader of the group.

"Boy," Dasch said. "I have a lot to talk to you [about], and I have to tell you something."

"I know what you want to do," Burger said.

"If you know," Dasch said. "You have to kill me."

Burger smiled. "I am quite sure that our intentions are very similar."

The restaurant was too crowded now to discuss anything more. Dasch said they would talk about it later.

The following morning, Sunday, June 14, Dasch ordered room service and invited Burger to join him. They ate their bountiful breakfast without any meaningful conversation.

Afterward, Dasch pushed the room service cart out into the hallway. When he returned, he shut the door behind him and locked it. He threw the room key into the bathtub and walked over to the window. He pushed it open, looked down the thirteen stories, and turned around to face Burger.

"We are going to have to talk," Dasch said. "And if we don't agree with each other, only one of us will leave this room alive."

What was said between the two men, no one will ever know for sure. But what was clear to each of them was that their mission, Operation Pastorius, had been compromised from the moment they ran into the coast guardsman. Not to mention Dasch's lost notebook, which could lead the authorities right to him. Dasch revealed that he had worked out a new plan. But it required an accomplice, so Dasch had to trust that Burger would be on board.

Burger had never liked or trusted Dasch, and it crossed his mind that Dasch might be leading him into a trap. But Burger had defied death under the Nazi regime twice. So he knew how to play his hand, whether Dasch was sincere in what he was about to tell him or not. Furthermore, there was one major factor pushing them into a shaky alliance. Fear.

Dasch confessed that he was going to turn himself in to the FBI. That said, Dasch still wanted to do and be something bigger and better. And he believed Operation Pastorius was a chance for him to be a hero to his country. But he claimed that his loyalties were divided. So instead of being loyal to Germany or America exclusively, he chose both.

Dasch reasoned that if he called the FBI and turned

himself in, he would be a hero to the American people for stopping Hitler's secret attack on the United States. He saw himself as another William Sebold, the Nazi spy who became famous for destroying Hitler's spy ring in America by turning into a double agent. At the same time, Dasch figured he would be helping the German people who wanted to be free from the Nazi regime. Dasch intended to propose a plan to the FBI to "lick the Nazis with their own weapons" by helping America with their propaganda campaigns against the Nazi regime, the impact of which, Dasch thought, would result in the overthrowing of Hitler's regime. Dasch maintained that he had always planned on turning himself in from the moment he realized returning to Nazi Germany was a mistake, which was soon after his arrival. After revealing his true identity and his plan, he asked Burger what he thought about their situation. Burger's answer was short and risky.

"I do not intend to carry out the orders," Burger confessed. "I left the cigarette box, the bottle, the raincoat, and all the small items [of clothing] in the sea bag on the beach where we landed from the submarine. It is probable that by this time the boxes have been found and it will be impossible for any of our group to immediately carry out any of the orders given to us by Kappe, because all of the manufactured explosives we brought with us have in all probability been seized."

But neither of them was sure what to do next. They worried that Quirin and Heinck were suspicious of Dasch because he hadn't overpowered the coast guardsman. And Burger was worried that the Gestapo had infiltrated the New York office of the FBI. At the same time, he didn't want to get arrested before voluntarily informing the FBI.

Dasch wanted to wait long enough for the second group to arrive. He reasoned that everyone, especially Herbert Haupt, should have a chance to come forward and turn themselves in. Their discussion was interrupted when they realized it was approaching noontime, and they were scheduled to meet Quirin and Heinck at the Suisse Chalet.

Dasch picked up the phone and asked for the Hotel Chesterfield. He wanted to tell Quirin and Heinck they were running late. But the hotel operator told Dasch that neither Quirin nor Heinck was staying there. Dasch didn't know where they could be or how to reach them, raising his suspicion that Quirin and Heinck didn't trust him and Burger.

Dasch and Burger spent the rest of the afternoon trying to figure out how to handle their dangerous situation. They finally decided they would call the FBI, but first they hailed a taxi and went to Grant's Tomb on Riverside Drive for the prearranged meeting with Quirin and Heinck. It was 6:20 p.m. when they arrived. They were twenty minutes late.

They saw Quirin and Heinck sitting on a bench. Quirin and Heinck were relieved to see them, fearing something terrible had happened to Burger and Dasch. But they were still feeling angry and nervous at the

pair. Even so, their faces did not betray any recognition of them. They stood up and started walking toward Columbia University. Burger and Dasch followed closely behind them. When they crossed Broadway, Dasch and Burger joined them.

Quirin couldn't hide his feelings any longer, and he looked noticeably "peeved." He didn't like that they'd been kept waiting not only at Grant's Tomb but also at the Suisse Chalet restaurant. He wasn't going to tolerate this behavior.

"Kappe's orders were for us to move on to Chicago as soon as possible," Quirin spat, challenging Dasch's leadership.

"I have some important conferences coming up," Dasch retorted. "And we will all have to stay in New York City until I am ready to leave."

As their leader, Dasch explained that his important business was to take care of "the correctness and sufficiency" of their forged identification papers.

"I will have to leave New York in order to contact some people," Dasch told them.

The only point that everyone understood and agreed upon was that it was too risky to go back to the beach for the explosives. But no one knew what to do about it. So nothing was planned.

For now, Quirin was worried about the cost of his hotel room, at a rate of $5.50 a night ($85.33 in today's dollars). He also didn't feel safe there. Dasch asked them which hotel they were staying in, and Quirin lied, telling him the Chesterfield. That was the hotel Dasch had called earlier when he discovered they weren't registered there. Quirin's lie confirmed to Dasch that they didn't trust him. So when Quirin asked Dasch where they were staying, Dasch lied and said the New Yorker Hotel.

Before the meeting broke up, Heinck complained about his money belt. He was extremely worried about carrying around so much cash. In fact, he was afraid to wear it. So Dasch offered to take the money off his hands. Heinck opened his money belt and took out five hundred dollars. He handed the rest over to Dasch, and felt some relief. His constant fear of being arrested was only growing with each passing minute. But, at that moment, he felt more reassured about Dasch as the head of their team. So Heinck offered him his hand. Dasch reached out and clasped it, shaking it up and down. Heinck told him that he trusted him as their leader. Dasch still thought Heinck was a loudmouthed coward. But he kept his opinion to himself.

After the meeting was over, Dasch and Burger took a bus back to their hotel. Dasch was nervous, "all tied in knots." Even so, he went to a phone booth, looked through the directory, and found the number to the local FBI. Dasch slid the glass door shut, pushed some coins into the slot, and dialed the number.

FBI agent Dean McWhorter was sitting by the phone in the New York office when it rang. He had been assigned to work the "nut desk" and didn't know who to expect on the other end of the line. McWhorter was tasked with fielding all types of calls, usually from angry, crazy, and/or drunk citizens.

So when he answered the ringing phone, and the man on the other end of the line told him to make a record of the call, he did. But McWhorter didn't take it seriously. When he asked the man for his name, he couldn't understand what the man on the phone was saying. So he asked him to spell it.

"F-r-a-n-k. D-a-n-i-e-l. P-a-s-t-o-r-i-u-s."

McWhorter still wasn't sure how to spell the name,

but he did his best. He then asked the caller what kind of information he wanted to share. The man told McWhorter that he had arrived from Germany two days ago and was going to see Mr. Hoover, the director of the FBI, in person in Washington, DC. The caller told him to alert the FBI in Washington. He said that he could be recognized by his distinct streak of gray hair.

McWhorter figured it was another prank phone call, exclaiming, "Yesterday, Napoleon called!" Even so, after he hung up, he followed procedure, writing the following memo:

> *Please be advised that at 7:51 p.m. on this date, Frank Daniel Postorius [sic] called this office by telephone, and advised the writer that he had made the call for the purpose of having a record of it, in this office. Postorius advised that he had arrived in New York City two days ago from Germany. He would not reveal his present address in the city, and remained uncommunicative concerning any information that he might be able to furnish this office. He stated that he was going to Washington, DC, on Thursday or Friday of this week, and would talk to Mr. Hoover or his secretary.*

He refused to come to this office and report his
information and said that he had to see a certain
person in Washington first, but he wanted this
office to make a record of his call and to notify our
Washington office that he was coming there. This
memo is being prepared only for the purpose of
recording the call made by Postorius.

The memo was filed away and forgotten. No one thought it was worth forwarding to the FBI in Washington.

Two days later, on Wednesday, June 17, a German U-boat surfaced off the coast of Florida in Ponte Vedra, near Jacksonville. Four Nazi saboteurs landed and buried four boxes of explosives. No one noticed.

Chapter 6

TRUE LIES

Two days later, Friday, June 19, 1942
Washington, DC

Whenhen George Dasch woke up in the swanky Mayflower Hotel in Washington, DC, he tried not to worry. The hotel was a five-minute walk from the White House and the favorite lunch spot of J. Edgar Hoover, the director of the FBI. But Dasch didn't know that.

After he woke up, ate breakfast, and showered, he put on an expensive new suit. It was nearly ten o'clock, and he was ready to make his second phone call to the FBI. It had been five days since he had first notified them, and during that time, Dasch's fear and anxiety had gotten the best of him. He was "a mental and nervous wreck."

Dasch had dealt with his nerves by gambling. He played cards for thirty-six hours straight before he left New York, winning a couple hundred dollars. During that time, the saboteurs in his group didn't know what had become of him. And when he didn't arrive at a pre-arranged meeting at the automat, Heinck and Quirin were furious. Any trust Heinck had felt toward Dasch as their leader evaporated.

By now, Quirin and Heinck expected Dasch to have firm plans about their trip to Chicago and definite answers about their next move. They wanted to get out of New York as soon as possible. Burger tried to reassure them, but he could see that "they were getting nervous and were becoming more suspicious" of Dasch and him.

When Dasch finally returned to the Hotel Governor Clinton from his gambling binge, he went directly to bed and slept. When he woke up at noon on Wednesday, June 17, Burger told him that Quirin and Heinck were "sore" with him and suspicious. But Dasch didn't want to deal with them, so Burger was once again left with the job of alleviating the anger and distrust that was fracturing their group.

As expected, the news of Dasch's gambling binge did not go over well with Quirin and Heinck, and they spewed out "profane language continuously" for the next forty-five minutes. Quirin was so furious that he wanted to take over as the leader. But Burger deftly handled the situation, smoothly spouting off some lies in an effort to calm them down.

"George is planning to leave New York City for a couple of days in order to make some important contacts," Burger said. He followed it up with, "George has already made preparations for us all to go to Chicago."

Burger's lies were convincing, and Heinck and Quirin believed him. For the time being.

When Burger returned to his hotel, he found that he also had to soothe Dasch's anxiety. So he talked over their plans and reassured Dasch about their decision. Burger reminded him that they hadn't done anything against the United States, and by going to the FBI, they were doing everything in their power to prevent the men from committing any acts of sabotage.

The following morning, on Thursday, June 18, Dasch felt ready to go to Washington, DC. In preparation, he went out shopping and bought a leather briefcase. Upon returning to his hotel room, he counted the dollar bills that were stashed away in his old suitcase. He tallied $80,000, then added the cash from his money belt. He placed the money in envelopes and carefully repacked it into his newly purchased briefcase. He sat down at the desk, pulled out some hotel stationery from the drawer, and wrote a note.

> *Content $82,350*
>
> *Money from German government for their purpose, but to be used to fight Nazis.*
>
> *George J. Dasch, alias George J. Davis, alias Franz Pastorius.*

Before leaving for Washington, DC, Dasch had left a note behind for Burger, telling him, "You may rest assured, that, I shall try to straighten everything out, to the very best possibility . . . If anything extra ordinary should happen, I'll get in touch with you directly." He signed it, "I'm your sincere friend, George."

Now, Dasch was in Washington, DC, and he was finally ready to call the FBI for a second time. So, he picked up the phone and dialed.

FBI agent Duane Traynor was a calm, methodical, and observant professional. He was also a hard worker. As the head of the FBI's antisabotage unit, he worked six days a week, most evenings, and sometimes, he even worked on Sundays. His sabotage cases typically involved disgruntled employees threatening to sabotage their employers. When Agent Traynor's phone rang on Friday, June 19, and he picked it up, he was not expecting someone like George Dasch to be on the other end.

Dasch started the conversation by telling Traynor that his name was George Davis, and he was the leader of eight men who had just arrived from Germany. Dasch asked to make an appointment to speak to someone about sabotage, preferably J. Edgar Hoover.

Traynor thought Dasch was a "crackpot—clown" on the other end of the line. But it was his responsibility to investigate, so he offered to meet with him at his office. Dasch wasn't sure how to get there, so Traynor sent some agents to pick him up.

It was almost eleven o'clock when Dasch walked into Traynor's office. When Dasch removed his hat, Traynor noticed his distinct gray streak of hair. He also noticed that Dasch was all dressed up in expensive clothes. Traynor himself followed the FBI's dress code; he was sporting a white shirt and dark suit. Like the other FBI agents, Traynor favored a snap-brim hat.

Dasch was visibly nervous, explaining that lives were at stake. He asked Traynor if the FBI in New York had sent him the message regarding his first call. Traynor had no idea what Dasch was talking about. But his boss had told him the strange story about the landing of German agents on Long Island and how the Coast Guard had run into a man with a streak of gray hair. The "crackpot—clown" with the streak of gray hair sitting before him suddenly had Traynor's full attention.

Dasch informed Traynor that he had been through "considerable mental strain and hardship" and he had a long story to tell but he only wanted to tell it in his own way. Traynor told him to tell his story, and he was willing to listen. Dasch started at the beginning, revealing that he came to the United States from Germany.

"Did you come by submarine?" Traynor asked, figuring he had the right to ask questions.

"I won't answer that kind of question," Dasch said, making it clear that he was only going to tell what he wanted. At least at first.

So Traynor listened while Dasch "rattled on" about how he'd first arrived in the US as a stowaway, how he had worked as a waiter, and how he had joined the U.S. Army and was stationed in Hawaii. Traynor kept listening, and when Dasch finally started talking about coming over on a submarine, Traynor tried to find out every detail.

Dasch's story closely matched coast guardsman John Cullen's version. He also mentioned their training at Hitler's sabotage school and how the focus of the mission was to sabotage war production in the United States. Furthermore, Dasch expressed his regret in returning to Nazi Germany almost as soon as he arrived, and how he had worked on figuring out a way to return to the United States.

"It became clear to me that this whole set-up of Nazism has to be fought," Dasch told Traynor. "I had to find a way to do it. In the country itself I was unable to do any effective work. So, therefore, I had to find a way to leave the country."

Dasch explained his desire to help the United States fight the Nazis, not with guns, but with propaganda. If the right type of propaganda was directed at the German people, he believed the Nazi regime could be overthrown.

Traynor listened patiently to Dasch, who emphasized that he was supplying information to the FBI as a means toward that end—to fight against Hitler and his "rotten gangsters." But Traynor pointed out to Dasch that the FBI had two primary objectives.

The first objective was defensive. The FBI wanted to locate anyone who was planning "to blow up and damage any part of our war industry in this country." The second objective, which Dasch was more interested in, was using propaganda to fight the enemy.

Dasch expressed his willingness to cooperate with the FBI regarding any defensive measures. He wanted to help the FBI capture the other saboteurs.

Traynor believed that Dasch was being sincere in his willingness to help. But Dasch wouldn't divulge any details regarding the whereabouts of the other saboteurs. Instead, Dasch talked about his own plan to capture them.

Dasch's plan was for him to go back to his group and act as if everything was the same. He was scheduled to meet with Kerling and his group, and he would lead the FBI to all of the saboteurs at once. If all went according to Dasch's plan, he would be a hero. But that wasn't how it worked out.

——

A few floors above Traynor's office, FBI Director J. Edgar Hoover was receiving summarized reports on Traynor's interview with Dasch, who was described as a "temperamental individual." The good news was that Dasch had "taken a shine" to Traynor.

Hoover thought Dasch was withholding information so that he would have leverage over the FBI and would be considered indispensable. This didn't sit well with Hoover, who had his own plan on the best way to capture the other saboteurs. And it did not involve Dasch being a hero.

But he needed Dasch to talk and give them the whereabouts of the other men. That was Traynor's job.

It was nearly four o'clock in the afternoon on June 19 when a taxicab drove down the leafy tree-lined street in Chicago, Illinois. The cab pulled over and parked; Herbie Haupt paid the driver, stepped out, and shut the door. Clutching his new leather suitcase, he rang the doorbell and waited.

After landing near Jacksonville, Kerling, Thiel, Neubauer, and Haupt had spent one night in Florida, then they split up. Haupt was to go home to Chicago and make contact with his uncle, Walter Froehling. Kappe had ordered him to enlist his uncle to help them with developing a network of people to assist them in creating terror and panic.

His uncle's address on Whipple Street was written in invisible ink on a handkerchief carried by Kerling. The twin was carried by Dasch. There was no question that his uncle would help the men. Kappe knew Froehling's brother, Otto, a barber in Germany, was in a concentration camp for saying something he shouldn't have while he was cutting a customer's hair. Kappe instructed Haupt to tell his uncle Walter about his brother's imprisonment and warn him that his cooperation was the only way to help his brother get out of the concentration camp.

Despite Haupt's own predicament, at this particular moment, he was just happy to be back in Chicago after a long train ride. He wanted to see his family. When the front door finally opened, Haupt saw his aunt Lucille. She was completely surprised to see him at her door. The last time anyone had heard a word from him was when he was in Japan. She immediately asked him if he'd been home to see his parents. Haupt shook his head and said, "No." He was worried about his mother,

Erna. He explained that the sudden shock of seeing him might upset her.

His aunt told her husband to call Haupt's mother, which Walter did right away. But instead of telling Erna that her son was back in town, he told her that his wife, Lucille, was sick. Haupt's mother said she'd come over immediately.

When Haupt's mother arrived, he hid in a bedroom while his uncle broke the news that her beloved son was back home. She rushed to him, wanting to know how he was. She could see that his hair was neatly cut and he was wearing an expensive new tan suit and a flashy new wristwatch.

Haupt told his mother, aunt, and uncle about his travels to Mexico, Japan, and Germany. He even told them that he arrived in the United States on a submarine. At first, no one believed him, but when he gave them news about their relatives in Germany, they were convinced.

At seven o'clock, when Haupt's father was finished with work, his mother called him and urged him to hurry over to the Froehlings' home. But that was all she said. So when he arrived, Haupt's father, Hans, was completely surprised to see his son. Herbie retold his story about traveling to Mexico, Japan, and Germany and returning to America on a U-boat. Then he opened his suitcase and pulled out a zipper bag. Inside the bag, hidden in a false bottom, he showed them thousands of dollar bills. It was more money than any of them had ever seen in their lives.

Even though Kerling didn't trust Haupt, especially with money, he had given him $20,000 (over $300,000 in today's dollars) to carry to Chicago. Haupt was instructed to hand it over to his uncle for safekeeping. It was a leap of faith on Kerling's part to expect Haupt to do as he was told.

But Kerling's risky decision paid off. Haupt asked his uncle to keep the money for him and to hide it on top of the mantel in their dining room, stating that under no circumstances should his uncle give the money to anyone but him.

Haupt didn't explain what the money was for. However, he did mention that there were three other men who came back with him on the submarine. One of the men was going to call him on his uncle's phone this Sunday at one o'clock.

Haupt's family understood that he "was working for the German government in some capacity." But they didn't know that he was to commit sabotage with bombs.

Nevertheless, his uncle, Walter Froehling, took the money and told Haupt he would help him. Haupt never mentioned that his brother, Otto, was in a concentration camp. Instead, he lied, telling him that his brother was still running a barbershop.

Although his mother was happy to see her son, she was "paralyzed with fear." His family was worried he was going to get caught. He tried to reassure them, telling them that he had been "schooled." But that didn't help assuage their fear. His family knew that he was "up to no good."

When he told his father that his job was to "hinder production," his mother scolded him, "You are here to do something against the country and here we are earning our living here."

With the money bag now in his uncle's hands, Haupt and his parents left the Froehlings at eleven o'clock and went home. Haupt wanted nothing more than to go directly to bed. His parents' constant badgering was starting to irritate him, and he told them he didn't want to talk about it anymore. But they ignored his complaint and informed him there was one more problem to solve. While he'd been away, the FBI had stopped by and was looking for him. They wanted to know why he hadn't registered for the draft.

At eleven o'clock in Washington, DC, on the same night, Dasch was still talking. He and Traynor were now on a first-name basis. Dasch had even given Traynor the nickname "Pie," a reference to baseball player Harold Joseph "Pie" Traynor of the Pittsburgh Pirates.

Traynor was trying to "take advantage of all the opportunities to advance trust" with Dasch, so he would reveal important details. That meant removing any barriers and using any psychological tools at his disposal, such as using nicknames to create a sense of friendship.

While Dasch was busy talking to Traynor, FBI agents were dispatched to Dasch's room at the Mayflower Hotel. They secretly searched his room and looked for any evidence that supported Dasch's story. When they discovered his new leather briefcase, they picked the lock and uncovered the enormous amount of cash he had stored inside. They also found the porcupine-shaped pin that Dasch had made for his group while on the U-boat. The agents carefully put everything back, just as they'd found it, before leaving the room. Now they knew Dasch was the real deal—a Nazi saboteur.

At eleven thirty that night, after talking for more than twelve hours, Dasch was finally ready to give Traynor his first lead in the case. He told them that Peter Burger could be found at the Hotel Governor Clinton in New York City.

The next day, Saturday, June 20, Peter Burger left his hotel room at about two thirty in the afternoon. He hadn't heard from Dasch since he'd left for Washington, DC. He had expected to receive some word from George or the FBI, but heard from neither.

What Burger didn't know was that Dasch had written him another letter. In the letter, Dasch informed Burger that he had indeed arrived safely, had contacted the right individuals, and was trying hard to do the right thing. Dasch asked a hotel employee to mail it for him, but the FBI had intercepted the letter.

Burger also didn't know that the FBI was tailing him when he walked out of the hotel and down the street that day. He was on his way to Rogers Peet clothing store near Fifth Avenue and Forty-Second Street. Burger was going to pick up some new clothes there, and he was also going to meet up with Quirin and Heinck.

For the past two days, Burger had tried to keep Quirin and Heinck distracted. But it was proving to be more and more difficult. The first night Dasch was away in Washington, Burger and Quirin shimmied and grooved at a roaring jazz club on New York's famous Fifty-Second Street. They didn't get back to Burger's hotel room until the wee hours of the morning.

Quirin went back to Burger's hotel and got a room. But their good times turned bad when Quirin woke up and finally noticed his luxurious accommodations. When he met Burger in his room for breakfast, he began another argument, protesting that their choice of a deluxe hotel would draw attention to them. But, perhaps worst of all, he insisted that Dasch and Burger "were not living up to the orders" given to them in Germany. They should be moving forward with their plan and well on their way to Chicago.

"I will not stand for what is going on," Quirin seethed. "George and you will have to suffer the consequences."

Quirin left without saying goodbye and went back to the cheap boardinghouse where he and Heinck were now staying. Burger was left with a growing fear that his life was in danger. The saboteurs had all been instructed to kill any team member who acted suspiciously, to ensure that no one would destroy the mission.

So on Friday night, June 19, Burger met up with Quirin and Heinck for dinner. His intent was to curb their independence by keeping a watchful eye on them. After dinner, they returned to Burger's hotel room.

Burger went into the bathroom to change his clothes. While he was standing in front of the bathroom mirror, he saw Quirin open the drawer to his desk. Burger remained quiet while he watched Quirin remove the note that Dasch had written to him before leaving for Washington, DC. He continued to remain calm and quiet while Quirin read it, then handed it over to Heinck. No one said a word, and the note was returned to the drawer. But Burger was unnerved.

Burger dressed hurriedly and ushered the group out of the hotel, hoping to avoid any questions or harm from Quirin and Heinck.

Everyone acted like nothing had happened as they set off for another night on the town. They hailed a taxicab and drove off "to meet some chance girl acquaintances."

They stayed out all night. In the early hours of the morning, they went their separate ways and Burger returned to his hotel room. They had all agreed to meet later that afternoon at Rogers Peet clothing store, where they were scheduled to pick up their newly tailored clothes.

If Heinck and Quirin were upset about Dasch's letter to Burger, they covered up their feelings. No mention was made of it at their meeting. Everyone acted calm and cool. But hidden underneath the tranquil surface was a maelstrom of fear and suspicion.

After picking up their new clothes, they grabbed a bite to eat. They paid the bill, shook hands, and said goodbye. Burger went back to the Hotel Governor Clinton, still unaware that the FBI was following him.

Quirin and Heinck took a bus uptown. Little did they know, two FBI agents were riding with them. They all hopped off at Broadway and Seventy-Second Street. Two FBI cars were nearby. While Heinck went into a drugstore, Quirin kept walking up Amsterdam Avenue. It was 4:30 p.m. when FBI agents apprehended him and shuttled him off in a car to FBI headquarters.

Heinck was the next one to be arrested. From the drugstore, he had walked to a deli, and as he was leaving, the FBI nabbed him.

Meanwhile, Burger was back in his hotel room. It was nearing five o'clock, and he was trying on his new sharp-looking sharkskin suit. After looking in the mirror, he sat down and started reading the newspaper. When he heard the commotion at his door, he didn't bother to get up to open it. He'd left it unlocked. When the FBI charged into his room, Burger wasn't surprised. He'd been waiting for them.

The FBI arrested the saboteurs separately, so they wouldn't know anyone else had been caught. They also interrogated them separately to compare stories and sift through the lies to find the truth.

Burger fully cooperated. The FBI noted that he seemed "100% against Germany." Heinck confessed not long after the interrogation started. Quirin was the least cooperative, trying to use his cover story as he was instructed back in sabotage school. But when it dawned on him that the FBI knew all about Operation Pastorius, he confessed.

What the FBI didn't know yet was where to find the

other four saboteurs. Fortunately, Dasch was still talking.

It was eleven o'clock on Saturday night, June 20, and while the first team of saboteurs were being interrogated by the FBI, Haupt's parents drove him over to the home of Wolfgang Wergin, his friend and traveling companion whom he had left behind in Germany. Haupt wanted to deliver the message to Wergin's parents that Wolfgang was all right and sent his love. He told them about their adventures to Mexico, Japan, and Germany. He mentioned that he came home on a submarine. But he didn't mention that he'd attended sabotage school. Even so, everyone understood that he was working for the German government.

Wolfgang's father informed Haupt that he had done something similar for Germany during World War I. And he offered to help. Following that, Haupt confessed to them how their son was being used as leverage to ensure that Haupt completed the assignment. He tried to assure them that Wolfgang wasn't being held by the Gestapo yet. But if Haupt didn't follow Kappe's orders or he went to the FBI, the Gestapo would most likely arrest and imprison Wolfgang.

The Wergins were distraught that something so terrible could happen to their son. The Haupts and the Wergins continued to talk, and Haupt expressed his concern about registering for the draft. The Wergins and his parents advised him to register immediately. They reasoned that if he registered for the draft, then the FBI wouldn't have any desire to question him. They needed him to be careful, so that their son would be safe.

Haupt and his parents finally left the Wergins' at four o'clock in the morning. Mr. Wergin warned Haupt to "watch out for a 'tail'" and to stay away from his house. He didn't want Haupt leading anyone, especially the FBI, to him.

Before leaving, Haupt pressed a fifty-dollar bill into Mrs. Wergin's hand. He knew they had financial worries. He told her it was from her son. Mrs. Wergin knew that was a lie. She knew that her son didn't have fifty dollars to give her. But she kept it anyway.

Afterward, his parents dropped Haupt off at the Froehlings' house. Haupt was expecting a call. The following day, Sunday, June 21, at noon, the phone rang. It was Hermann Neubauer. They agreed to meet in an hour and a half at a movie theater where *The Invaders* was playing, a film about men who land in a rubber boat from a submarine and invade the United States.

After the movie, they went next door to a restaurant. Neubauer was so nervous that his stomach was upset. But he forced the food down anyway. Ever since he'd been injured in the war, he was a nervous wreck. Since arriving in Chicago that morning, he couldn't shake off the feeling that he was being watched.

"I get excited about every little thing very easily," he revealed. "And any noise makes me nervous."

Neubauer told Haupt about his train trip to Cincinnati with Kerling and Thiel. He described how everyone acted and how they were afraid to ride in a taxicab. Then he disclosed the details of a prearranged meeting between the leaders of the first two teams of saboteurs.

The plan was for Kerling and Dasch to meet in Cincinnati on July 4 to discuss their next moves. Afterward, Kerling would travel to Chicago and meet up with Haupt. Together, they would drive down to Florida to retrieve the explosives that were buried in the sand. The only problem with the plan was that gasoline was being rationed. So traveling to Florida by car was likely out of the question. But that was Kerling's problem as the leader to figure out.

Another problem Kerling was working on, Neubauer told Haupt, was whether they should go through with the sabotage plans at all.

Neubauer had never been happy about being assigned to the mission. When he found out that he was going to the United States as a saboteur, he didn't like the idea at all. His wife was American and, although she'd moved to Germany with him, her parents still lived in America. And he didn't think highly of saboteurs.

Even so, Neubauer believed he had no choice about his assignment. Since Kappe was a lieutenant, and Neubauer's superior, he felt obligated to follow his orders.

Besides, Neubauer was afraid for his American wife. The police were constantly harassing her and questioning her about why she didn't work and why she didn't have a baby. She was frightened and worried about being treated like a criminal.

He feared that if he were caught, his wife would pay for it. "They naturally would have taken my wife to a concentration camp," Neubauer said. "And she would never have a chance to get away from Germany . . . I was afraid of that."

When he and Kerling had taken the train to Cincinnati, they noticed that the railroad stations, the railroads, and the factories they passed were well guarded. They had discussed whether it was even possible to commit acts of sabotage. As the leader, Kerling tabled the decision, reassuring Neubauer that it would be discussed later when the group was reunited in Chicago on July 6. Kerling wanted it to be a group decision. And if they decided to abandon the mission, Neubauer and Kerling planned to escape to either Mexico or Canada. But if that wasn't possible, they would all go to the FBI together and turn themselves in.

When Neubauer finished giving Haupt the update, he asked Haupt what he had been doing since he arrived home. Haupt still didn't trust Neubauer and didn't want him to know how much he'd revealed to his family. So he lied and told him that his family and friends thought he had just returned from Mexico.

Later that night, Wolfgang Wergin's parents went over to the Haupts' home. "The Froehlings, Wergins, and my mother and father were extremely worried about what was going to become of me and all of them were of the opinion that I should immediately register with the draft board and get a job."

On Monday, June 22, Haupt listened to his parents and friends and went to the draft board and the FBI. He had no idea that George Dasch had already confessed, and that everyone in Dasch's group had been arrested.

Chapter 7

THE BETRAYED

Monday, June 22, 1942
Washington, DC

While Haupt was registering for the draft, the FBI was trying to figure out his whereabouts. Although Dasch had already given the FBI the names of all the saboteurs and their descriptions over the weekend, he honestly didn't know when they were to land in Florida or where they would go after they arrived. But he was willing to reveal more details about his prearranged meeting with Kerling and the others.

That said, Dasch refused to reveal more to Traynor before receiving certain assurances. Dasch wanted to make sure that the other men didn't know that he was the person who had betrayed them. He and his family could be killed if they found out. Traynor liked Dasch, and he knew Dasch's information was critical to the FBI's success in capturing the saboteurs. So he shook Dasch's hand, promising to protect his part in taking

The Betrayed

down Operation Pastorius. Traynor didn't realize at the time that it was a promise he couldn't keep.

Dasch told Traynor that they were to all meet at the Gibson Hotel in Cincinnati on July 4. If the FBI waited, Dasch would lead them to Kerling and his group. Dasch tried to reassure the FBI that no sabotage would take place prior to the meeting. But the FBI didn't want to take such a big risk.

"[Is] there some way you could communicate with Kerling?" Traynor asked Dasch.

Dasch knew only one way.

"We jotted down different addresses on hand-kerchiefs," Dasch said. "One of which is in my possession now."

Dasch showed him the plain white handkerchief and told him about the invisible ink. "Lieutenant Kappe bothered the hell out of me to give him some reliable address in the United States through which he could always reach me."

Dasch explained that he had given Kappe a fake address. But Kerling hadn't lied. All the addresses on Dasch's handkerchief were correct.

"If it's in secret ink, how do we find out what's on it?" Traynor asked.

147

It was a good question. One that Dasch couldn't answer.

"If I had known you boys were going to ask all these questions," Dasch said, "I would have learned it all good, so I could tell it to you."

Privately, the FBI agents wondered if Dasch was withholding information. However, he did tell them that whatever chemical they had used to reveal the invisible ink had smelled awful. Traynor sent the handkerchief to the FBI's lab, hoping they could figure it out.

But the day before, on Sunday, June 21, Dasch suddenly remembered the name of the malodorous chemical.

"Ammonia," he exclaimed. "I passed the handkerchief over a bottle of ammonia . . . it shows red until it dries. You read it slowly and then it goes away again. You have to do it slowly. Just pass it over ammonia water."

Today, on Monday, June 22, the FBI lab used ammonia on the handkerchief. Like magic, four names and addresses appeared, then disappeared. One of the names was Helmut Leiner.

"He is a very good friend of Kerling . . . We agreed that any time I lost track of this Kerling guy, I should always get in touch with Leiner. He would tell me where this Kerling is to be found," Dasch said.

Another name on the handkerchief was Walter Froehling, Herbie Haupt's uncle.

Within minutes, local agents in Chicago and New York were dispatched and on their way.

Same day, Monday, June 22, 1942
Chicago, Illinois

While FBI agents raced to the home of Herbie Haupt's uncle, Herbie had already gone to the draft board and registered, and was in a taxi on his way to the FBI office in Chicago. When he arrived, he was greeted politely and taken to an office where he met an agent.

The agent asked Haupt where he'd been for the past year. He told the FBI that he had just returned from Mexico, where he'd been prospecting for gold. He didn't tell them about his trips to Japan or Germany. Haupt showed the agent his draft card and mentioned that he had participated in the Reserve Officers' Training Corps (ROTC). The agent was satisfied with Haupt's story. Or so Haupt thought.

Before he left, the FBI agent had one more question. Was Haupt willing to go to war for the United States?

"I would rather not fight against the German people," Haupt replied truthfully. "But if I had to go, I would go." That was a lie.

The FBI agent told Haupt that he could go. So Haupt left the building and hailed a yellow cab. He was home in time for lunch. Later he went to his favorite bars, visited friends, and got his old job back at Simpson Optical. He had no idea that the FBI was following him the whole time, hoping that he would lead them to the other saboteurs.

On that same Monday afternoon, Eddie Kerling, the leader of the second group of saboteurs, was busy in Central Park. He and Werner Thiel had traveled together to New York City, where Kerling wanted to take care of some business.

After contacting his friend, Helmut Leiner, whose name and address Dasch's handkerchief had revealed to the FBI, he arranged a meeting with Hedy Engemann. Hedy was the girlfriend Kerling had left behind when he returned to Germany. During his time away, he had come to the realization that she was the woman of his dreams. And he was willing to take any risk to see her.

When Hedy first saw Kerling in the park, she was

completely "dumbfounded." She hadn't heard from him and had no idea he was coming back to America. But she was happy to see him. After they embraced, she asked him how he had managed to get back into the United States.

"Ask me no questions and I will tell you no lies," he said.

The only thing he did reveal was that he had traveled across the Atlantic in a submarine. Hedy didn't ask many questions, and he didn't tell her much more. But he did express his undying love for her. She felt the same way about him.

"I loved him so and could not find the strength to leave [him]," she later said.

Kerling asked her if she wanted to go on a road trip with him to Cincinnati, Chicago, and Florida. While describing the trip, he left out an important detail. Kerling didn't tell her that he was going to Florida to pick up explosives. So Hedy also didn't realize that she'd just been recruited to assist Kerling in his mission to commit acts of sabotage. Unwittingly, she said, "Yes!"

There was just one problem he needed to clear up. Kerling wanted to tell his wife, Marie, about their plans. No one expected it to be a problem because they had been separated for a long time. In fact, Hedy was good friends with her. They both shared in "the same heartache."

So when Kerling's friend Leiner arranged a meeting for him with his wife, Hedy agreed to join them.

The following evening, Tuesday, June 23, Kerling shared a cab with his friend Leiner. They had spent the day in Newark, New Jersey, trying to find a pro-Nazi minister named Emil Krepper, whose name was written in invisible ink on his handkerchief. But they couldn't track him down.

So they returned to the city and ate dinner in Times Square. While at the restaurant, Leiner called Kerling's wife, Marie. At first he only told her that he wanted to set her up on a "blind date," but she refused. So Leiner finally revealed that her husband was back in town and planned on being there. Marie immediately agreed to meet at 10:30 p.m.

Kerling was also scheduled to meet Thiel at a bar on Lexington and Forty-Fourth Street. So the cab pulled over, and Kerling said goodbye to his friend Leiner.

Inside the bar, Kerling saw Thiel and Anthony

Cramer, Thiel's good friend and a fellow Nazi supporter. Thiel hadn't told his friend all the details of their mission, but Cramer had guessed some of it. Thiel was planning to give his money belt to Cramer because he was too nervous carrying so much cash. Neither Kerling nor Thiel noticed the FBI agents sitting nearby.

After ordering drinks, they talked for a while, and when it approached ten o'clock, Kerling left. So did the FBI agents, following Kerling down Lexington Avenue. They watched him pace as he waited anxiously to meet his wife. But Kerling wouldn't be there for the reunion. The FBI agents arrested him.

Not long after, Thiel was arrested. And so too were Thiel's and Kerling's friends: Helmut Leiner, Anthony Cramer, and Hedy Engemann.

On the day of Kerling's arrest, Tuesday, June 23, Herbie Haupt spent the morning at home with his mother, blissfully unaware that the FBI was on his tail. Haupt talked to his mother about Gerda Stuckmann, the girl-friend he'd left behind a year ago. He hadn't had to tell his mother about Gerda's pregnancy because she already knew about it. Soon after Haupt had driven off for Mexico, Gerda had stopped by the house and told his mother. But Haupt learned that the baby had died a few days after being born.

Haupt told his mother that he wanted to rekindle his relationship with Gerda. But he'd sent her only one post-card during his time away. He wrote it when he made a stop in St. Louis during his cross-country trip. Gerda hadn't heard a word from him since. So he asked his mother to call her and smooth things over for him. His mother agreed, dialing Gerda's phone number.

"Herbert's back," she told Gerda. "But he doesn't say anything. I don't know where he's been. All I know [is] that he's terribly nervous."

When his mother asked Gerda to meet her for lunch, Gerda accepted the invitation. When Haupt's mother returned home, she told her son that Gerda was excited and wondered if Haupt wanted to see her. He did. So he called Gerda himself and invited her to come over that evening.

In the meantime, Haupt took some money out of his money belt and placed $2,500 in a brown envelope. He went into his parents' bedroom and hid it under the rug. He told his father about it.

With the rest of his cash in hand, Haupt asked his

father to come shopping with him. He wanted to buy a car. Even though gas was rationed, Haupt was supposed to drive Kerling down to Florida to pick up the boxes of explosives that the second team had left behind after landing. Kerling had instructed Haupt not to buy a car, but Haupt wanted one. And he was certain he had figured out a loophole. He was going to buy the car in his father's name so if he was arrested, his father could keep the car. It was a shrewd idea. But it wasn't intelligent. Haupt didn't consider the possibility that the loophole would be incriminating, not only to him but also to his father.

Later that day, Gerda arrived at the Haupts' home. She noticed immediately that Herbie was nervous. She thought it was because he hadn't registered for the draft. But then he told her that he had registered and commented that the FBI was "awfully nice" to him.

When Gerda asked him where he'd been for the past year, all he would say was, "I've been through a lot." When she asked him how he got back to the United States, he wouldn't say anything. Gerda had a "hunch" that something was wrong. But she didn't press him for details.

After dinner, Haupt and Gerda went out for a drink

together. Still unaware that the FBI was watching his every move, he surprised Gerda with a marriage proposal. He handed her ten dollars so she could pay for the blood test that was required for a marriage license.

Gerda was confused. She didn't understand why he wanted to marry her now. A year ago, when they spoke of marriage, he'd left town in a hurry. Despite her nagging doubts, she said, "Yes!"

When he called her the next day, Gerda told him that she had taken the blood test for the marriage license. She asked him if he had taken it too. Haupt told her he had, but he was lying.

Haupt asked to see her that night. But Gerda told him that she wasn't available until Saturday, figuring, "If there was something wrong, they'd have him by then."

The following day, Thursday, June 25, Haupt was supposed to start his job at Simpson Optical. But when he woke up, he lied to his mother that he wasn't feeling well.

After calling in sick, he hopped into his newly purchased car and drove off to meet his friend Bill Wernecke, a fervent Nazi supporter and an expert draft dodger. The FBI followed.

Wernecke was surprised to see Haupt, telling him he had thought he was in Japan.

"No, I have been in Mexico and South America and had someone send the cablegram for me from Japan," Haupt lied. He didn't trust Wernecke, but he needed his help to avoid the draft.

During their conversation, the subject of registering for the draft came up. Haupt told him he had registered a few days ago. Wernecke thought Haupt would probably be drafted right away, but he offered a solution.

"He said he would take me to a doctor for an examination," Haupt said. "And that I should tell the doctor that I had coronary thrombosis, rheumatic pains, swelling of my ankles, pain in my left upper arm, dizzy spells now and then, headaches every week, indigestion, pains in my chest, and pains in my back. According to Wernecke, no doctor in the world could tell whether my heart was bad or not."

Wernecke knew firsthand because he had received a draft deferment for a physical disability. He had faked deafness, rheumatism, and heart trouble. Wernecke knew which doctor to take him to: Dr. Otten, a Nazi sympathizer. They drove to his office at 3856 South Parkway.

When Dr. Otten asked what was ailing Haupt, Wernecke rattled off Haupt's "symptoms."

"We'll fix him up!" Dr. Otten replied.

After that the doctor took Haupt's pulse and blood pressure, which was high.

Haupt told him, "I had a fever in Mexico and had been taking quinine."

The doctor thought that was most likely what caused Haupt's heart to act up, but, other than high blood pressure, Dr. Otten thought his heart was all right. When he left the room, Wernecke told Haupt to ask for a cardiograph. So he did, and Dr. Otten ordered one.

"He gave me some pills to aid my digestion and help me sleep," Haupt said. "And I told him I would be back after having the cardiograph."

Before leaving, Haupt asked the doctor for a signed note to give his employer, advising against any physical exertion until a diagnosis was determined. Dr. Otten wrote it out on his prescription pad and handed it to him. There was no charge for the appointment. It was Dr. Otten's contribution to the Nazi regime.

Later, while Haupt and Wernecke were driving down an empty road, they noticed a car following them. They stopped their car, and the car behind stopped. They turned their car around and drove by the suspicious car. There were two men in white shirts and dark suits in the front seat. But when the suspicious car turned off the road, Haupt and Wernecke figured they were wrong. And there was no one on their tail.

The following day, Friday, June 26, Haupt and Wernecke went to the drugstore to buy nitroglycerin pills. Afterward, they drove to St. Joseph's Hospital so Haupt could have a cardiograph. Before his examination, Haupt went outside and swallowed three nitroglycerin pills to make his heart beat rapidly.

"Bill [Wernecke] had told me that they should be taken about fifteen minutes before," Haupt said. So the palpitation would show up on the graph.

When Haupt was called in for the cardiograph, Wernecke followed him.

"While I was lying on the table, Wernecke stood behind a door and made faces and motions to indicate to me that I should hold my breath and beat my chest," Haupt said.

Haupt couldn't beat his chest because a nurse was standing nearby, but he did hold his breath. When the exam was over, Haupt paid the five-dollar fee and made an appointment to pick up the results the next day.

But Haupt wouldn't arrive for his appointment. On Saturday, June 27, while Haupt was driving his new car to pick up his cardiogram results, the FBI arrested him. They also arrested his mother, father, aunt, uncle, and Wolfgang Wergin's parents.

There was only one Nazi saboteur still at large, Hermann Neubauer. The FBI had no idea where he was. For days, they had kept a close watch on Herbie Haupt, leaving him alone to see if he would lead them to him.

During that time, Haupt had met Neubauer once, on Wednesday, June 24, but unbeknownst to Haupt, he'd accidentally shaken the FBI off his trail.

When the FBI interrogated Haupt, he at first denied knowing anything about Operation Pastorius. But he did admit to knowing Neubauer, and shared the name of the hotel where he thought Neubauer was registered.

When the FBI went to the deluxe hotel, Neubauer was long gone. But the FBI had a system in place to aid their search.

"Every hotel in town was to report the names of everybody that was registered in their hotel every night," FBI agent Duane Traynor explained. "The agents got the lists from those registrants. They were looking for Neubauer, or his code name of Nicholas."

FBI agents were assigned to go to every hotel in Chicago. They dashed from hotel to hotel, scanning the list of names in the registration book and looking for the name "Nicholas." It was a tedious task, and it wasn't until several tries that they finally found one where a "Nicholas" was registered.

They raced up to the room, banging on the door. But no one answered. They rushed back to the lobby and found the hotel manager. He ran with them to the room and opened the door. The FBI quickly searched the room for clues.

They rifled through the drawers and opened the closet. They wouldn't find the nearly $4,000 Neubauer was given for the mission. He had entrusted it to friends who were hiding it in a coffee can on a shelf in their kitchen pantry. But there were other clues.

"They found all brand new clothes, all [with] Jacksonville labels on them . . . So they were pretty sure they had the right man," said Traynor.

The FBI waited confidently for Neubauer's return. And at 6:45 p.m., the door to his room opened, and

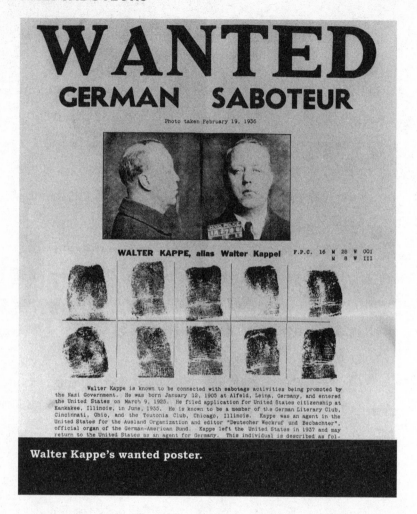

Walter Kappe's wanted poster.

Neubauer, unaware, walked right in. The FBI slapped on the handcuffs and arrested the last Nazi saboteur.

Hitler's secret attack on America was thwarted.

PART THREE

Life or Death

Chapter 8

BEHIND CLOSED (AND GUARDED) DOORS

Same day, Saturday, June 27, 1942
Washington, DC

"**Y**ou sure took chances," the FBI agents told Dasch, over and over again. They thanked him for the invaluable information he provided. They couldn't have rounded up and arrested the saboteurs without it.

Dasch felt like a hero. And when he was asked to show up in prison so the other saboteurs would know that everyone was caught and the mission was dead, he complied. The suggestion made sense to him. Dasch didn't want the other saboteurs to know that he was the one who'd double-crossed them. It never entered his mind that someone might double-cross him.

Later that day, FBI director J. Edgar Hoover announced to the public that German U-boats had landed eight highly skilled Nazi saboteurs on America's shores. But "almost from the moment the first group set foot on United States soil" the FBI was in hot pursuit. Hoover assured the American public that the explosives were seized and the saboteurs imprisoned.

Hoover didn't mention any help from the Coast Guard or George Dasch in cracking the case. He lied to protect the stellar image of the FBI. He and President Roosevelt wanted Hitler to believe that American spies had infiltrated the German sabotage school and the German Army. The president wanted his enemies to think that America's defenses were impenetrable. He also didn't want the Nazis to know how they were able to capture the saboteurs so quickly.

The following day, on Sunday, June 28, Dasch was escorted to New York and taken to the federal court building. They asked him to change out of his new suit and wear a prison uniform. Afterward, his mug shot was taken. Dasch still didn't understand that he was being placed under arrest.

He was led past the prison cells of all the Nazi saboteurs, with the exception of Burger, who already knew about Dasch. The men got a good look at him before he was locked in a cell and left there.

Hours passed, and yet Dasch kept thinking, "Those fellows should be coming to get me out of here soon."

On Sunday, June 28, the news of the Nazi saboteurs and their capture was broadcast on American radio. Across the ocean, at a German listening post, an *erfasser*, or a radio monitor, listened to the news and translated it from English to German. When the news of the failed mission reached Hitler, he launched into a violent tirade. "Why didn't you use Jews for that?" he screamed.

After thirty-six hours alone, the door to Dasch's cell was unlocked and he was taken to a room to speak to two FBI agents. One of them was Duane Traynor.

"I am very upset," Dasch said. "I didn't expect to be left all this time alone in a cell."

Traynor greeted him in his usual friendly manner. And Dasch asked if he was going to be let out of prison.

"Look George, Mr. Hoover and all of us know that you have performed a great service for our cause and we know that you did a courageous thing," Traynor said. "We have expressed our thanks to you many times. And you have our admiration too. But George, you will now have to master another great job. You must become an actor."

Traynor explained that to fool Hitler, Dasch would have to be tried along with the other saboteurs. It was the only way to keep Dasch's involvement in their arrests a secret. The FBI wanted him to plead guilty.

"The trial was to be held in federal court," Dasch stated. "And if I were to contest the case, my whole story would come out and one of the most valuable aspects of the incident would be ruined."

Dasch didn't want the news getting back to Germany that he was the turncoat. He was concerned that his family living in Germany would be killed. Plus, he didn't want the other saboteurs to know that he was the traitor.

"I am here to assure you that your pleading guilty before the court does not mean that you were actually guilty . . . It is primarily an expedient necessity to keep your part in this case away from the Nazis," Traynor explained. "After the excitement has blown over and not more than six months after the trial, you will be freed with full presidential pardon and complete exoneration of all charges on which you will be tried."

Dasch didn't like the idea of pleading guilty. But he understood why they needed him to comply, so he agreed. The FBI stressed it was also for the security of his parents and family who were still living in Germany.

"Yes, sure," said Dasch. "For the security of my parents, I am willing to do that."

Before leaving, they shook hands. Dasch was taken back to his prison cell. In front of Traynor, he had been calm. Now he was visibly upset and began pacing in his cell. The guard outside his door could hear Dasch talking to himself.

"I've been a coward, but tonight I found myself."

The guard continued to listen. "Young people should live. People who have already lived their lives can die. That's the way my mother and father would want it."

Dasch was too upset to sleep much that night. But it wasn't until the next morning that he truly understood that he wasn't going to be the hero of the story. As he peered through the slit in the wooden door to his cell, Dasch saw a guard sitting in a chair reading the newspaper. The front page was facing Dasch, and he could read the blaring headline: "CAPTURED NAZI SPY." Underneath the headline was a photo of him.

Dasch was in shock. "Am I accused of being a spy?" he wondered to himself. It didn't make sense to him.

But there was his picture in the paper. The FBI had promised him this wouldn't happen.

Feeling betrayed, Dasch worried how the news would affect his family, especially his American wife. He broke out in a cold sweat.

Soon after, he told the FBI that he wasn't going to lie and plead guilty. Dasch was going to risk retribution for a chance to tell his story in federal court.

The FBI was infuriated. And it was at this point that FBI agent Duane Traynor began to doubt his first impression of Dasch. In the beginning, Traynor believed that he was being sincere in wanting to help. He liked Dasch and thought he was very personable and very talkative. But he also thought Dasch was unstable and high-strung with grandiose ideas of himself.

In a memo, Traynor had described Dasch's complex personality.

> As an egomaniac, he likes to picture himself in two characters, one of George John Dasch and the other of George John Davis. George Davis is a stool pigeon, an informer and a traitor to the German government. [This] is the individual who is furnishing all the information in this case and who

immediately reported his landing to the FBI in
order that no sabotage would occur and no lives
would be lost. On the other hand, George Dasch is
the individual who is fighting for the German
people, the true people of Germany who are
opposed to the things that Hitler stands for. He
believes these people to be in the majority in
Germany at the present time but feels they are
coerced into following Hitler's methods and
program.

Before Traynor began to waver, others had doubts about Dasch's motivation in coming forward to confess. In a government report, a military lawyer, who studied Dasch's statement to the FBI, wrote: "In almost every criminal prosecution of groups of men, one or more of them will attempt to save his own skin either after his complicity has been discovered or when he feels reasonably certain that it will be discovered, by coming to the prosecuting officials and telling a part of the story. One may always be certain that anyone who will sell out in an effort to secure either exemption from prosecution or leniency will minimize in every way possible his participation in the offense."

But Lord Rothschild, a spy with MI5 (Britain's homeland security), who also analyzed the information, believed Dasch. He acknowledged that "DASCH's character is difficult to fathom." Even so, in his official report, he stated that "It is abundantly evident that the leader of the first group of saboteurs, George John DASCH, had every intention of giving himself up to the American authorities and compromising the whole Expedition, probably from the moment that it was first suggested to him in Germany that he should go to the USA on a sabotage assignment."

Even though the FBI needed Dasch to plead guilty to keep everything a secret, it ultimately wasn't going to matter. Dasch didn't hold the power. President Roosevelt did.

President Roosevelt was going to send a powerful message to Hitler. He wanted the Nazi saboteurs executed. However, if they were tried in a civilian court, the men would most likely receive a two-year prison term for conspiracy, since they didn't commit any sabotage. But under military law, the men could be charged with violating the rules of war. Since the saboteurs traveled on enemy submarines, secretly crossed the front line,

President Franklin Delano Roosevelt.

brought explosives, and disguised themselves in civilian clothes, under military law, they could be considered spies and sentenced to death.

So, on July 2, President Roosevelt issued a proclamation to establish a military tribunal under the Military Code of Justice.

> *Whereas, the safety of the United States demands*
> *that all enemies who have entered upon the*
> *territory of the United States as part of an invasion*
> *or predatory incursion . . . should be promptly*
> *tried in accordance with the Law of War . . . all*

> *persons who are subjects, citizens or residents of*
> *any nation at war with the United States . . . or act*
> *under the direction of any such nation . . . and are*
> *charged with committing or attempting or*
> *preparing to commit sabotage, espionage, hostile or*
> *warlike acts . . . shall be subject to the law of war*
> *and to the jurisdiction of military tribunals.*

The military tribunal would be composed of seven generals to serve as the judges, with President Roosevelt presiding over the proceedings. As the commander in chief of the armed forces, the president would have the sole power to review the final verdict.

A military tribunal differs from civilian court in several ways. It's closed to the public and media, so secrecy is assured. The rules regarding admissible evidence are more lenient, allowing hearsay, or rumors. The verdict does not have to be unanimous among the judges, and appeals are not guaranteed.

The president's proclamation was a thorny maneuver. Military tribunals weren't supposed to be used when civilian courts were functioning. In fact, there hadn't been a military tribunal for civilians since Abraham Lincoln's assassination trial. The outcome had resulted in the hanging deaths of one woman and seven men for conspiring with assassin John Wilkes Booth in Lincoln's death.

Military tribunals are also controversial because they deny the accused the right to habeas corpus. This allows the accused the opportunity to make the government prove to a judge that their arrest and imprisonment is justified. The legal rule is in place so the police and government can't abuse their power and lock someone up for no reason.

FBI agent Duane Traynor agreed with the president's decision. He reasoned that secrecy was critical. The United States wanted Hitler to think that there was a "mole" inside the Nazi regime. So if Hitler sent anymore saboteurs to America, he would fear that the mole would let the FBI know, and that mission would be thwarted too.

After the Japanese bombing of Pearl Harbor and their invasion of Alaska, Americans wanted a victory. "This is no time to be squeamish," the *Chicago Daily News* reported. "This case is one for martial law and military tribunals, no matter who made the arrests. The people expect stern action, fully publicized by radio to the entire world. Americans are not softies, and they certainly do not want more spies here by ill-timed leniency."

On July 4, 1942, while most Americans were celebrating Independence Day, the Nazi saboteurs were transferred to a jail in Washington, DC, under the custody of the army. Upon arrival, a doctor examined each prisoner and asked if he had any complaints. Despite the bruises on the bodies of Kerling and Thiel from their interrogator, who had resorted to beating them to get them to confess, no one complained.

Afterward, the prisoners changed into their uniforms and were taken to their tiled cells. The cells on each side of them were empty, and each saboteur was kept in solitary confinement. They weren't allowed to see or talk to anyone other than their lawyer.

Precautions were taken so the prisoners couldn't escape or harm themselves. The lights in their cells were always on, day and night. At mealtime, a guard watched over each prisoner while he ate. The food was served on paper plates, and they ate with paper utensils.

They weren't allowed to see any family or friends, and they were forbidden to speak to one another. Dasch felt utterly hopeless and fearful. He was "going crazy from desperation and frustration."

When the military tribunal began on July 8, 1942,

the prisoners changed into the new clothes that they purchased on their shopping sprees. Under armed escort, the saboteurs were transported to the Department of Justice. For days they had been insulated from the outside world and the reporting on their capture. Now the men were shocked by the public outrage against them.

"We are watched more carefully than vicious criminals," Heinrich Heinck wrote to his wife. "Handcuffs, machine guns, and so forth. The sirens scream loudly when we ride through Washington. You know what I think of America but now my dream and ours has been destroyed."

After the prisoners arrived at the Department of Justice, they entered in the basement and were taken into a specially reserved elevator, which stopped on the heavily guarded fifth floor.

With the exception of Dasch, who asked for his own lawyer, the other saboteurs were assigned to Colonel Kenneth Royall. Although Royall didn't like the idea of representing enemies of the United States, he took his job seriously. And, most important, he wanted a fair trial for them. So his first argument was that the Nazi saboteurs should be allowed access to civilian courts.

"In deference to the commission and in order that

we may not waive, for our clients, any rights which may belong to them, we desire to state, that in our opinion, the order of the President of the United States creating this court is invalid and unconstitutional," Royall said.

The attorney general, Francis Biddle, disagreed. The defendants had no civil rights because they were "exactly and precisely [in] the same position as armed forces invading this country."

The generals took a recess to discuss the argument while the saboteurs waited anxiously, knowing that their lives were at stake. After forty-five minutes, the generals-judges returned. "The Commission does not sustain the objection of the defense."

So the military tribunal continued, and the list of criminal charges they were accused of were listed.

1. Breaking into the United States defense zone and hiding within that zone

2. Planned sabotage

3. Spying

4. Conspiracy

J. Edgar Hoover (center) sits among the military commission

If convicted, the saboteurs could be sentenced to death.

For the next few weeks, until July 27, the lawyers called witnesses to testify, and argued the case. Dasch, Burger, Haupt, Heinck, and Quirin each swore they never intended to go through with the sabotage plan. Thiel and Neubauer said they were just following orders. Kerling insisted that he didn't think the mission was going to be a success and wanted to escape to South America, where the Nazis were "running the show."

The saboteurs' lawyer knew their best defense was to have the case transferred to a civil court. So, after closing arguments, Colonel Royall quickly sent an appeal to the Supreme Court (which would later be known as the Quirin case). In a last-ditch effort to save the Nazi saboteurs' lives, Royall referred to the Milligan case from the Civil War, which states that as long as the civil courts are open, defendants are entitled to a civil trial. He argued that it set the precedent. Therefore, the saboteurs should be tried in civilian courts.

Three days later, the Supreme Court rejected the appeal, denying them the right to habeas corpus. The Supreme Court ruled that "the spy who secretly and without uniform passes the military lines of a

Haupt and Dasch with a guard in between them during the trial.

belligerent in time of war, seeking to gather military information and communicate it to the enemy, or an enemy combatant who without uniform comes secretly through the lines for the purpose of waging war by destruction of life and property . . . [are not] entitled to the status of prisoners of war . . . [and are] subject to trial and punishment by military tribunals."

A few days later, on August 3, the generals at the military tribunal reached a verdict: death for all eight saboteurs. Their verdict was reviewed by President Roosevelt.

Early Saturday morning, on August 8, the prisoners were told their fate. The president had ordered execution by electric chair for Herbie Haupt, Heinrich Heinck, Eddie Kerling, Hermann Neubauer, Richard Quirin, and Werner Thiel. He spared the lives of George Dasch and Peter Burger. Dasch was sentenced to thirty years in prison, and Burger was sentenced to life in prison.

"As I told each of the six condemned of the decision and informed him the sentence would be carried out that morning, he turned pale and seemed stunned, but not one of them spoke a word to me," said their jailer Albert Cox. "Dasch, sentenced to thirty years, gasped out his fears that his family in Germany would be punished."

Dasch was so distraught he wrote a letter to President Roosevelt. He refused to believe the verdict and emphatically denied that he had committed any of the crimes he was charged with, nor did he ever intend to commit any crime. He demanded his freedom, writing, "I have rightly earned such liberty by beating Hitler at his own game and thereby have saved the people of the United States loss of life in addition to destruction."

Dasch never heard back from the president.

In the meantime, preparations were being made for the electrocutions. Trained executioners were hired. A bag of salt was sent for from the kitchen to be mixed into a solution that would be applied to the prisoners' legs and partially shaved head. Electrodes, which are conductors of electricity, would be placed on the skin in those areas.

At 10:00 a.m. the prisoners were taken from their current cells and moved to their "death" cells. Once there, their hair was clipped and partially shaved, and their pants were slit on their right leg. The men were also allowed to write a final letter.

Herbie Haupt was scheduled to be the first one executed. He wrote a farewell letter to his girlfriend, Gerda, telling her that he came back to America for her. He had meant to make it up to her and his parents. "But I brought nothing with me but *Horror* for my Parents and trouble for you," he wrote. "I have managed to put my Mother, Father, and Uncle into jail, decent People who never have done a thing wrong in their life."

At 12:01 p.m. Haupt was taken into the execution chamber. He was strapped down to the chair. At 12:03 a current was applied. Eight minutes later, he was pronounced dead.

Heinck was next, followed by Kerling, Neubauer, Quirin, and Thiel. After each execution, the dead body was taken to the basement under guard. At 1:25, two ambulances arrived at the jail. Two hours later, the bodies of the dead saboteurs were taken to the morgue. Soon after, they were buried in unmarked graves in a potter's field.

Years later, Dasch would finally learn why the commission had found him guilty: *"a last minute change due to fear when he arrived in the United States."* The commission reasoned that once the saboteurs ran into the coast guardsman, the fear of getting caught seized Dasch and changed his intentions.

But Dasch bitterly maintained that he had always planned on betraying the mission before his feet ever touched the sand in Amagansett. To Dasch, his intentions were clear and consistent in his actions, stating:

"My handling of the coast guardsman was decidedly contrary to orders . . . I left the shovel stuck in the sand above our buried explosives . . . I called the FBI . . . If I was afraid, why didn't I take the $80,000 and just disappear?"

Dasch vehemently denied that a fear of getting caught and a desire to save his own life played any role in destroying Hitler's secret attack on America.

"I know what fear is," Dasch wrote in his defense. "I felt it many times in Nazi Germany; I felt it many times when I thought of the risks I was taking in plotting the doom of the Pastorius mission . . . And one thing is certain, once I proceeded safely beyond the beach at Amagansett, all my fears left me. They didn't return again until jail doors clanked closed behind me."

Five years later, 1947

George Dasch was not a model prisoner. High-strung and unpredictable, the prison warden labeled him a "troublemaker."

The first three years were especially hard on Dasch. The government ordered him to be held as a "restricted or isolated prisoner" to keep him separated from the other inmates. For Dasch, it was the most depressing time of his life.

When Dasch was finally allowed to interact with the other prisoners, no one liked him. "He is a loquacious individual who likes to brag about his activities as an espionage agent and his connections with Nazis," the prison ward reported. "He goes out of his way to antagonize [other prisoners] by belittling their intelligence."

Dasch was bitter and angry about the outcome of his trial. He didn't think the trial was fair or honest.

Once Dasch was sentenced to prison, he stopped helping the government. Peter Burger, on the other hand,
was a model prisoner.

"His conduct here under very unfavorable circumstances has been exemplary," the prison warden wrote.
"He has been a diligent worker. He has cooperated with
me and the institutional officials in every respect, and
he has courage equal to any man I have ever known or
heard of. He is straight forward and I believe is honest
and has the interests of this country at heart."

Unlike Dasch, who was an overtalkative and irritat-
ing witness at his trial, the government had asked
Burger to be a witness at other trials. Risking the safety
of his family back in Germany, Burger agreed to help.

"He testified in a number of court cases which
resulted in convictions of saboteurs and espionage
agents practically on his testimony alone," the prison
warden wrote.

Burger testified in the treason trial of Herbie
Haupt's parents, Herbie's aunt and uncle (the Froehlings),
and the parents of Herbie's friend Wolfgang Wergin.
During the trial, Burger did not reveal how the FBI
tracked down the Nazi saboteurs, but he did give details
about Operation Pastorius. When the defense lawyer

asked him if the government promised him immunity for testifying, Burger said, "I may remind you, sir, that you are speaking to a German soldier. The U.S. Government respected me by not offering any promises. I expect the same of you, sir."

When the defense lawyer asked him, "Do you know where Herbert Haupt is now?"

Burger replied, "I understand he gave his life for his country."

The defense lawyer asked which country he was referring to.

"I meant my own country," Burger said. "Germany."

The Haupts, the Froehlings, and the Wergins were all found guilty. Herbie's father, uncle, and Wolfgang Wergin's father were sentenced to death. Their wives were sentenced to twenty-five years in prison and fined $10,000. Later, those sentences were overturned on appeal. The women were found not guilty, and Wergin and Froehling were sentenced to five years. Herbie's father was sentenced to life in prison. After the war, they were all deported to Germany.

And so were Dasch and Burger. In 1948, President Harry S. Truman agreed to suspend their prison sentences. One of the conditions of their release was that they were never allowed to return to the United States.

Although they were no longer prisoners, their betrayal of the other Nazi saboteurs would stain their freedom. When they finally arrived back in war-devastated Germany, instead of being welcomed home, they were called traitors. For the rest of their lives, they tried to conceal their part in Operation Pastorius. Dasch, in particular, was a target and often moved from town to town.

"Whole carloads of people . . . come around looking for me, some of them acquaintances or relatives of the six men who were executed," Dasch revealed. "Others were just patriotic Germans who wanted to get even with a 'traitor.'"

Dasch understood their anger toward him. The deaths of his fellow saboteurs were "very painful" to him. And he never wanted them to be executed. But he felt misunderstood.

"I would have given anything to have their lives spared," he stated. "But sadly enough, in a war people are killed. And in this war my sympathies were entirely on the side against Hitler. I had acted, not against the German people but against the Nazis. If enough other

Germans had done the same thing, they would have spared themselves and their nation a lot of misery."

September 11, 2001

On a clear, sunny day, nearly sixty years after Hitler's Nazi saboteurs landed on America's shores, nineteen terrorists hijacked four commercial passenger planes and carried out suicide attacks against the United States. Two fuel-loaded planes crashed into the World Trade Center in New York City, a third slammed into the Pentagon near Washington, DC, and the fourth crashed into a field in Pennsylvania. Nearly 3,000 people were killed.

Osama bin Laden, the leader and founder of the al-Qaeda terrorist organization, took credit for the coordinated attacks and reportedly funded them. For bin Laden, who despised the Western influence on the Middle East, his religion, Islam, influenced his political beliefs. He believed that all Muslims (followers of the religion of Islam) should rise up in jihad, or holy war, and create a single Islamic state. The terrorist attacks on 9/11 were allegedly a retaliation for America's support of Israel (territory that Jews consider their ancestral homeland while some Muslims consider it their land), its involvement in the Persian Gulf War (code-named Operation Desert Storm), and America's ongoing military presence in the Middle East.

Following the terror attacks, President George W. Bush said, "Whether we bring our enemies to justice, or bring justice to our enemies, justice will be done."

On November 13, 2001, President Bush issued an order to set up a military tribunal system to try the men accused of helping the hijackers. President Bush's order was closely based on former president Roosevelt's proclamation to try the Nazi saboteurs in a military tribunal. Similarly, the president was in charge of picking the judge, picking the jury, controlling the evidence, and controlling the rules. One major difference was that President Bush's order was wider in scope, to include anyone who was "not a United States citizen" that he had reason to believe is or was a member of al-Qaeda; has engaged in, aided or abetted or conspired to commit acts of terrorism; or has knowingly harbored an al-Qaeda terrorist.

A military tribunal is still a controversial issue. Prior to 9/11, terrorists were prosecuted in civilian courts. Some people argue that even if a person isn't a citizen of the United States, he or she should still have rights outlined in the U.S. Constitution.

In response to the terror attacks, President Bush repurposed the military base at Guantánamo Bay (also known as Gitmo) as a prison to detain suspected terrorists in the United States' "war on terror." Since Gitmo is leased land from Cuba, the prisoners are not on U.S. soil, so they are not covered by the U.S. Constitution. Also, each accused terrorist is considered an "enemy combatant" and denied some legal protection.

By 2003, five suspects were captured, interrogated, and tortured. It wasn't until 2008 that they were arraigned and charged with conspiracy, attacking civilians, attacking civilian objects, intentionally causing serious bodily harm, destruction of property in violation of the law of war, hijacking an airplane, murder in violation of the law of war, and terrorism.

Soon after their arraignment, newly elected President Obama suspended the case and considered trying it in a federal court in New York City. The idea was eventually nixed, and in 2012, the suspects were arraigned again. Seven years later, no date for the death-penalty trial has been set. The controversy surrounding military tribunals and civil rights continues.

And the impact of the Nazi saboteurs' mission to attack America lives on.

NAME

Khalid Sheikh Mohammed

NICKNAME

KSM

INVOLVEMENT

"I was responsible for the 9/11 operation—from A to Z," he said. KSM is accused of proposing the 9/11 attacks on the World Trade Center and Pentagon to Osama bin Laden, the leader of the pan-Islamic militant organization al-Qaeda, in 1996. KSM oversaw the operation and training of the hijackers in Afghanistan and Pakistan. He was arrested in 2003, and the CIA tortured him before he was transferred to Guantánamo Bay in 2006.

NAME

Walid bin Attash

INVOLVEMENT

He's accused of running an al-Qaeda training camp in Afghanistan where two of the hijackers were trained. In 1999, he traveled to Malaysia to study airline security. He was arrested in 2003.

NAME

Ramzi bin al Shibh

INVOLVEMENT

He is accused of helping some of the hijackers find flight schools, enter the United States, and finance the operation. He was arrested on September 11, 2002.

NAME

Ammar al Baluchi

ALSO KNOWN AS

Ali Abd al Aziz Ali

INVOLVEMENT

He's accused of bankrolling the hijackers' expenses, flight training, and travel to the United States. He is KSM's nephew. He was arrested in 2003.

NAME

Mustafa Ahmad al Hawsawi

INVOLVEMENT

He's accused of giving money and credit cards to some of the hijackers and helping them dress like Americans. He was arrested in 2003.

Sources

To research further about Operation Pastorius, I recommend starting with the MI5 report (the link to the document is listed in this section). It's a fascinating read, written by a British secret agent, and it gives a great overview.

To dig deeper into the Nazi saboteurs' version of events, their backgrounds, and motivations, an excellent starting point is "Correspondence, Part 1" (document link listed in this section), which summarizes the testimony along with the corresponding page numbers to the unabridged court testimony. The saboteurs' FBI statements can be found in the "Dasch & Burger Correspondence, Part 3" (document link listed in this section). Also of interest is "Correspondence, Part 2" (document link listed in this section), where the government picked apart the saboteurs' statements, looking for inconsistencies and trying to uncover the truth.

DECLASSIFIED GOVERNMENT DOCUMENTS

Court Transcripts from the Military Tribunal and FBI Records

The military tribunal court transcripts and the saboteurs' statements to the FBI can be found in the National Archives Catalog: https://catalog.archives.gov/id/2133139. Each document link is listed below.

Military Commission. "[Court Martial Case 334178 (German Saboteurs)] Volume I of XVIII, Transcript." National Archives Catalog (6121078). July 8, 1942. https://catalog.archives.gov/id/6121078. (Coast guardsman John Cullen's testimony regarding his encounter with George Dasch.)

——. "[Court Martial Case 334178 (German Saboteurs)] Volume II of XVIII, Transcript." National Archives Catalog (6121079). July 9, 1942. https://catalog.archives.gov/id/6121079.

——. "[Court Martial Case 334178 (German Saboteurs)] Volume III of XVIII, Transcript." National Archives Catalog (6121080). July 10, 1942. https://catalog.archives.gov/id/6121080. (Peter Burger's testimony and detailed background.)

——. "[Court Martial Case 334178 (German Saboteurs)] Volume IV of XVIII, Transcript." National Archives Catalog (6121081). July 11, 1942. https://catalog.archives.gov/id/6121081.

——. "[Court Martial Case 334178 (German Saboteurs)] Volume V of XVIII, Transcript." National Archives Catalog (6121082). July 13, 1942. https://catalog.archives.gov/id/6121082.

——. "[Court Martial Case 334178 (German Saboteurs)] Volume VI of XVIII, Transcript." National Archives Catalog (6121083). July 14, 1942. https://catalog.archives.gov/id/6121083.

——. "[Court Martial Case 334178 (German Saboteurs)] Volume VII of XVIII, Transcript." National Archives Catalog (6121084). July 15, 1942. https://catalog.archives.gov/id/6121084.

——. "[Court Martial Case 334178 (German Saboteurs)] Volume VIII of XVIII, Transcript." National Archives Catalog (6121085). July 16, 1942. https://catalog.archives.gov/id/6121085. (George Dasch's interview with the FBI.)

——. "[Court Martial Case 334178 (German Saboteurs)] Volume IX of XVIII, Transcript." National Archives Catalog (6121086). July 17, 1942. https://catalog.archives.gov/id/6121086. (George Dasch's interview with the FBI.)

——. "[Court Martial Case 334178 (German Saboteurs)] Volume X of XVIII, Transcript." National Archives Catalog (6121087). July 18, 1942. https://catalog.archives.gov/id/6121087.

——. "[Court Martial Case 334178 (German Saboteurs)] Volume XI of XVIII, Transcript." National Archives Catalog (6121088). July 20, 1942. https://catalog.archives.gov/id/6121088.

——. "[Court Martial Case 334178 (German Saboteurs)] Volume XII of XVIII, Transcript." National Archives Catalog (6121089). July 21, 1942. https://catalog.archives.gov /id/6121089. (Herbert Haupt's testimony.)

——. "[Court Martial Case 334178 (German Saboteurs)] Volume XIII of XVIII, Transcript." National Archives Catalog (6121090). July 22, 1942. https://catalog.archives.gov /id/6121090.

——. "[Court Martial Case 334178 (German Saboteurs)] Volume XIV of XVIII, Transcript." National Archives Catalog (6121091). July 24, 1942. https://catalog.archives.gov /id/6121091.

——. "[Court Martial Case 334178 (German Saboteurs)] Volume XV of XVIII, Transcript." National Archives Catalog (6121092). July 25, 1942. https://catalog.archives.gov /id/6121092.

——. "[Court Martial Case 334178 (German Saboteurs)] Volume XVI of XVIII, Transcript." National Archives Catalog (6121093). July 27, 1942. https://catalog.archives.gov /id/6121093.

——. "[Court Martial Case 334178 (German Saboteurs)] Volume XVII of XVIII, Transcript." National Archives Catalog (6121094). July 31, 1942. https://catalog.archives.gov /id/6121094.

——. "[Court Martial Case 334178 (German Saboteurs)] Volume XVIII of XVIII, Transcript." National Archives Catalog (6121095). Aug. 1, 1942. https://catalog .archives.gov/id/6121095.

——. "[Court Martial Case 334178 (German Saboteurs)] 1942 Saboteurs Case, Correspondence, Part 1." National Archives Catalog (6121096). https://catalog .archives.gov/id/6121096. (Legal brief of the case. Summarizes the testimony with cross-references to page numbers of full testimony.)

——. "[Court Martial Case 334178 (German Saboteurs)] 1942 Saboteurs Case, Dasch & Burger Correspondence, Part 1." National Archives Catalog (6121097). https://catalog .archives.gov/id/6121097.

——. "[Court Martial Case 334178 (German Saboteurs)] 1942 Saboteurs Case, Correspondence, Part 2." National Archives Catalog (6121098). https://catalog .archives.gov/id/6121098. (Inconsistencies in Burger and Dasch's statements to the FBI.)

——. "[Court Martial Case 334178 (German Saboteurs)] 1942 Saboteurs Case, Dasch & Burger Correspondence, Part 2." National Archives Catalog (6121099). https://catalog .archives.gov/id/6121099. (Newspaper articles.)

——. "[Court Martial Case 334178 (German Saboteurs)] 1942 Saboteurs Case, Correspondence, Part 3." National Archives Catalog (6121100). https://catalog .archives.gov/id/6121100.

——. "[Court Martial Case 334178 (German Saboteurs)] 1942 Saboteurs Case, Dasch & Burger Correspondence, Part 3." National Archives Catalog (6121101). https://catalog .archives.gov/id/6121101. (German saboteurs' FBI statements.)

——. "[Court Martial Case 334178 (German Saboteurs)] 1942 Saboteurs Case, Dasch & Burger Correspondence, Part 4." National Archives Catalog (6121102). https://catalog .archives.gov/id/6121102.

——. "[Court Martial Case 334178 (German Saboteurs)] 1942 Saboteurs Case, FBI Reports on Reporter Firms." National Archives Catalog (6121103). https://catalog .archives.gov/id/6121103.

—. "[Court Martial Case 334178 (German Saboteurs)] 1942 Saboteurs Case, Miscellaneous." National Archives Catalog (6121104). https://catalog.archives.gov/id/6121104.

CIA Files

Central Intelligence Agency. "Kappe, Walter." National Archives Catalog (26221532). https://catalog.archives.gov/id/26221532.

Central Intelligence Agency. "OSS—Memorandum on German Saboteurs Who, via Submarine, Landed on the East Coast of the U.S." CIA Library Electronic Reading Room. (CIA-RDP13X00001R000100170004-2). https://www.cia.gov/library/readingroom /document/cia-rdp13x00001r000100170004-2.

MI5 File

MI5. "German Saboteurs Landed in US from U-boats in 1942. Report of Operation." National Archives, Kew.1942. http://discovery.nationalarchives.gov.uk/details/r /C1160276. (British agent Lord Victor Rothschild was sent to Washington so he could write a report for British intelligence on the Nazi saboteurs. It's a great overview of the mission.)

BOOKS

Dasch, George J. *Eight Spies against America.* New York: Robert M. McBride Company, 1959.

Dobbs, Michael. *Saboteurs: The Nazi Raid on America.* New York: Vintage Books, 2004.

Fisher, Louis. *Nazi Saboteurs on Trial: A Military Tribunal and American Law.* Second Edition. Lawrence, Kansas: The University Press of Kansas, 2005.

Rachlis, Eugene. *They Came to Kill: The Story of Eight Nazi Saboteurs in America.* New York: Popular Library, 1961. https://archive.org/details/theycametokill006979mbp /page/n1.

NEWSPAPER AND MAGAZINE ARTICLES

Abella, Alex. "A Terrorist Hunt in Summer 1942." *Los Angeles Times,* January 12, 2003.

Baumann, Edward and John O'Brien. "The Enemy Within." *Chicago Tribune,* September 22, 1985.

Cahan, Richard. "A Terrorist's Tale." *Chicago Magazine,* February 2002. https://www.chicagomag.com/Chicago-Magazine/February-2002/A-Terrorists-Tale.

Cox, Albert L. "The Saboteur Story." *Records of the Columbia Historical Society,* Washington, DC, Vol. 57/59, 1957/1959.

Crowley, Carolyn Hughes. "Meet Me at the Automat." *Smithsonian Magazine,* August 2001.

Engemann, Christel. "The Case of Hedy Engemann." September 3, 2011. http://www.foitimes/internment/Engemann.htm.

Goldstein, Richard. "John Cullen, Coast Guardsman Who Detected Spies." *New York Times*, September 3, 2011.

New York Times. "Fifth Ave. Crowd Put at 2,500,000." *New York Times*, June 14, 1942.

——. "La Guardia Sees Only One Greater Parade: When the Boys Come Home Victorious." *New York Times*, June 14, 1942.

——. "Parade Prologue Tells War's Story." *New York Times*, June 14, 1942.

——. "Parade Sidelights and Shadows, Too." *New York Times*, June 14, 1942.

——. "Sold Tickets to Nazis: Amagansett Agent Says 4 Waited for Early Train." *New York Times*, July 17, 1942.

Statesville Record and Landmark. "Widow Fiance of Saboteur Says She Is Through." (Statesville, North Carolina), July 2, 1942.

Swanberg, W.A. "The Spies Who Came in from the Sea." *American Heritage*, Vol. 21, Issue 3, April 1970.

Wood, Lewis. "Lone Coast Guardsman Put FBI on Trail of Saboteurs." *New York Times*, July 16, 1942.

——. "3 Nazi Spy Leaders Are Sought by FBI." *New York Times*, July 26, 1942.

WEBSITES

Government Printing Office. National Commission on Terrorist Attacks Upon the United States. Aug. 24, 2004. http://govinfo.library.unt.edu/911/report/index.htm.

United States Holocaust Memorial Museum. Holocaust Encyclopedia. https://encyclopedia.ushmm.org.

Photo Credits

Index

Note: Page numbers in *italics* refer to illustrations.

Acknowledgments

This mission would have been impossible without a truly great team of operatives. My sincere thanks to Amanda Shih for her steadfast enthusiasm, speed, and sharp insights. Her perceptive questions helped guide me to the heart of the story. My thanks to Paige Hazzan, who wanted the story told. Many thanks to Jessica Regel, a special agent (couldn't resist). And a never-ending thank-you to my husband, Todd. Nothing feels impossible when he's on your team, cheering you on.

SAMANTHA SEIPLE is the author of the young adult narrative nonfiction books *Ghosts in the Fog: The Untold Story of Alaska's WWII Invasion*, a YALSA Award for Excellence in Nonfiction Nominee and a Junior Library Guild Selection; *Lincoln's Spymaster: America's First Private Eye*, a Junior Library Guild Selection; *Byrd & Igloo: A Polar Adventure*; and *Death on the River of Doubt: Theodore Roosevelt's Amazon Adventure*. She is also the author of the adult narrative nonfiction book *Louisa on the Front Lines: Louisa May Alcott in the Civil War*. She lives in Asheville, North Carolina, with her husband, Todd, and their tiny dog, Lucy.